THE MAKING OF THE
NEW REVISED STANDARD VERSION
OF THE BIBLE

Members of the Standard Bible Committee in June 1981 (with two doctoral students from Princeton Seminary who served as recording secretaries) on the steps of Speer Library, Princeton Theological Seminary. Front row from left: Lucetta Mowry, Walter Harrelson, William A. Beardslee, Bruce M. Metzger, Charles D. Myers, Jr. (student), Robert C. Dentan. Middle row: Bruce Vawter, Allen Wikgren, Reginald H. Fuller, George MacRae, Harry M. Orlinsky, Delbert R. Hillers, Demetrios J. Constantelos. Back row: Paul S. Minear, James A. Sanders, William A. Holladay, Alfred von Rohr Sauer, J. J. M. Roberts, Marvin H. Pope, Charles H. Cosgrove (student).

The Making of the
New Revised Standard Version
of the Bible

by

BRUCE M. METZGER
Chair, Translation Committee

ROBERT C. DENTAN
Vice-Chair, Translation Committee

WALTER HARRELSON
Vice-Chair, Translation Committee

WILLIAM B. EERDMANS PUBLISHING COMPANY
GRAND RAPIDS, MICHIGAN

ISBN 0-8028-0620-1

Contents

v

Contents

Preface

THE CHAPTERS in this book were written by three members of the committee of translators responsible for producing the New Revised Standard Version of the Bible, published September 30, 1990. We have addressed the book to the general public with the aim of helping the reader of the Bible to understand the main principles that guided the work of the Standard Bible Committee.

Readers will recognize that some of the material in these chapters is of general interest, while other material deals with matters on which many people are not informed. We have attempted, however, to write for the majority of English readers rather than for scholars. There will be ample opportunity elsewhere to discuss in the technical language of scholarship the various issues with which the translators have had to wrestle.

Three of these chapters have appeared elsewhere, and we hereby gratefully acknowledge the permission to reproduce them here. Chapters 1 and 4 were published in *The Princeton Seminary Bulletin*, n.s. 11, no. 3 (1990). Chapter 2 was published in *Religious Education*, 85, no. 2 (Spring

1990), and is reprinted by permission of the publisher, The Religious Education Association, 409 Prospect St., New Haven, CT 06511.

The undersigned has made slight editorial adjustments throughout the four chapters in order to remove instances of repetition; it is hoped that the few that remain will not prove to be annoying.

December 1990   BRUCE M. METZGER

— I —

The Story of the
New Revised Standard Version

ROBERT C. DENTAN

SOME MODERN versions of the Bible lay special emphasis on the fact that they are completely fresh translations, without ties to the conventions of the past. Good arguments can be advanced for that kind of approach. But however valid the arguments may be — and most of these versions are excellent in their own way — such is not the philosophy of the New Revised Standard Version (NRSV), nor was it that of the old Revised Standard Version (RSV) on which it is based. In contrast, the committees that produced these versions are, or were, proud to stand in the direct line of descent from the earliest translation of the Bible into modern English, that of William Tyndale in 1534, and its "authorized" successor, the classic and beloved King James Version of 1611. In spite of all the changes that have been introduced, the NRSV is a revision, not a new translation of the Bible. The first revision of the standard English Bible by a committee was the ("English") Revised Version of 1881-95; the second, the revision published by the American members of that revision committee

in 1901 and called the American Standard Version (ASV);
the third, the Revised Standard Version of 1946-57 (Bible
with the Apocrypha).

I

When I was a student in Dean Luther A. Weigle's class in
American church history at Yale Divinity School in the
spring of 1930 and heard him speak, in his pleasantly
enthusiastic way, of his hope that a revision of the ASV would
soon be available that would both conserve its considerable
virtues and correct its all-too-obvious faults, it could hardly
have occurred to me that one day a revision of *that* revision
would be published, and that I would be a member of the
committee that produced it. This is how it happened. In
1929 the International Council of Religious Education, later
to be merged into a department of the National Council of
the Churches of Christ, had entrusted the work on a possible
revision of the ASV into the hands of Dean Weigle and a
representative committee of scholars. Such a revision seemed
desirable not only because of changing tastes in English style
and the rapid advance of modern biblical scholarship but
also because of certain distinguishing marks of the ASV that
hindered its wide acceptance as a satisfactory successor to
the universally admired KJV, in spite of the superior intelligi-
bility of the ASV for the modern reader and its much greater
accuracy in rendering the ancient Greek and Hebrew text.

    The most obvious of these characteristics was the
universal use in the Old Testament of the proper name
"Jehovah," instead of "the LORD," to translate the Tetragrammaton, the Hebrew name of God. However correct

this practice might be in scholarly theory — for the word in Hebrew is indeed a proper name, not a title — it was disastrous from the point of view of the liturgical, homiletical, and devotional use of the Bible and was almost universally disliked. The other limiting feature of the ASV was a product of the same kind of over-meticulous scholarship. This was the attempt to reproduce not only the words but also, as far as possible, the word order of the original ancient text. The result was an English version that was frequently more awkward than even the KJV.

Dean Weigle's committee decided to revert to the use of "the LORD" to render the divine name, because the constant use of "Jehovah" grates on the ear and it is not, in fact, an accurate representation of the mysterious name of the God of ancient Israel. The RSV's philosophy of language was, on the whole, conservative. The style of the ASV was modernized and its awkwardnesses smoothed over, but there was an effort to preserve something of the dignity and strength of the older English versions. Many passages, such as Psalm 23, were retained from the KJV without significant change. In prayers and other matters addressed to the deity even the archaic forms ("thou," "hast," etc.) were kept.

When the complete RSV was published in 1952 (the Apocrypha being added in 1957), it achieved wide acceptance in the churches except for a few very conservative groups that objected to the occasional use, in the Old Testament, of the ancient versions or modern scholarly conjectures to "correct" the traditional Hebrew text. Despite the general success of its endeavors, the committee was not content to remain idle. Far from regarding its work as complete, it continued in existence under Dean Weigle's presidency and from time to time expanded its membership, both to maintain its existence in the face of inevitable deaths and resignations and to broaden its representative character. (I became a member in 1960.) Every two or three years, under call of the chair, the committee would meet for extended sessions to consider suggestions that had been made for the improvement of the version and on occasion to deal with extensive agenda that had been submitted by church bodies. Every proposal was carefully examined and filed for use in a possible future revision. Some minor changes were eventually made in the Old Testament, and a second edition of the New Testament appeared in 1971.

II

Dean Weigle was one of those rare people who are vigorous and resilient at 90, but eventually, in 1966, it became necessary for someone else to assume the leadership of the committee. The new chair was Professor Herbert G. May of the Graduate School of Theology at Oberlin College in Ohio. With his accession to the office, the meetings of the RSV committee, which had previously taken place for the most part at Yale Divinity School, were transferred to the Oberlin campus, where they remained until 1976, when they began to be held at Princeton Theological Seminary.

In 1974 the National Council of Churches had authorized work to begin preparing a new revision of the Standard Bible which, it was optimistically hoped, would be ready for publication "sometime in the early 1980s." One could hardly have believed that the preparatory work would last through that entire decade so that the actual publication date would be deferred to the fall of 1990.

The decision to produce a further revision of the RSV was basically due to the social changes that took place during the sixties and early seventies. One of these was the tendency, whether for good or ill, toward less formality in social relationships, a relaxation of manner and dress that led inevitably to the use of a less formal style of language in public worship, sometimes almost to the point of colloquialization. Even in the stiffest of traditions it brought about the use of normal twentieth-century literary style in place of the archaic forms that had for many generations characterized the language of worship. What finally made this movement irresistible was the decision of the Roman Catholic Church to translate its Latin liturgy into English, and into current English rather than into an artificial liturgical style.

The RSV had already moved a long way in this direction by translating the Bible into contemporary English *except,* as was noted above, for speech addressed to God. In such passages (most of the Psalter, for example) the "thee's" and "thou's" were retained. For a full generation this had seemed a satisfactory compromise, as is evident from the fact that it was adopted for the New English Bible when it was published in the late sixties and early seventies. But by the time the decision was reached to revise the RSV all were agreed that the middle way was not good enough. After all, the KJV made no distinction between speech to God and speech to human beings, and neither did the ancient languages in which the biblical books were originally written. The RSV compromise had been a halfway step that demanded eventual completion; in the early seventies the time had obviously come for the committee to begin this necessary, though relatively mechanical task.

A second, and much more important, impetus for

reconsidering the style of the RSV was given by the wide-spread demand that the English language be purged of what seemed to many to be "sex-biased" language, notably the word "man" in the so-called generic sense that covers both men and women, and the indefinite "he," referring to an antecedent that might be either male or female. Many other examples are easily found. There is a large constituency, even of women, that feels such concerns are trivial, but the leaders of the mainline churches, both men and women, are committed to the use of "inclusive language," as are most younger women and most publishers and educational organizations. The movement in that direction is increasing and is not likely to be reversed. For a committee of scholars this general tendency in modern language usage is strongly reinforced by the fact that the sex-biased forms are, for the most part, accidents of English style and are not supported by the ancient biblical languages.

All in all, the committee had no doubt that this was another compelling reason for reexamining the text of the RSV, although it would obviously require a great deal more effort than was involved in merely updating obsolete language. It should be noted, incidentally, that the committee was never seriously tempted to change the allegedly patriarchal terminology the Bible uses about God — such terms as "Father," "Lord," or "King" — since these are inherent in the biblical text and in the thought-world of biblical times, not mere accidents of English style. The Bible is a historical document, and the function of the scholar is to transmit the ancient text as faithfully as possible, not to adapt it to contemporary tastes. The whole subject of inclusive language in the NRSV is treated at length in another chapter (pp. 73-84).

Once the need for modernizing the residual archaic

forms in the RSV and of purging the language of sex-biased elements had been recognized, it was evident that the time was ripe for a further revision of the entire text, having in mind the incorporation into the Bible of the results of the committee's thinking about the problems of biblical translation over a whole generation and the conclusions of contemporary scholarship. Scholars are constantly engaged in studying matters that are relevant to a proper understanding of the meaning of biblical passages. From time to time new manuscript evidence comes to light, grammarians arrive at a new understanding of Greek or Hebrew constructions, social studies illuminate the context in which ancient words were used, inscriptions and other discoveries in archaeological "digs" provide a new look at items in the Hebrew or Greek vocabulary, and scholars in library stacks get sudden flashes of insight that cause everyone to take a new look at passages they had always thought to be troublesome. The generally accepted conclusions of such study need to be incorporated in the biblical text for the edification of the general public. This provided a third motive for revising the RSV and gave the committee a third area in which to operate.

Even in the context of scholarship in the forties and fifties, the original RSV was something of a compromise, as all "authorized" versions necessarily are. The 23rd Psalm is a rather extreme illustration. In the RSV text the psalm appears essentially in its KJV form, but with footnotes that give alternative translations. In at least three of these instances scholars almost universally regarded the alternatives as preferable, but these were relegated to the margin while the familiar KJV language was retained in the text ("right paths" vs. "paths of righteousness"; "the valley of deep darkness" vs. "the valley of the shadow of death"; "as long as I live" vs. "for ever"). By the seventies this kind of deference to tradition was no longer necessary, especially since several new translations incorporating the marginal readings had already appeared. The committee now had the opportunity to bring the RSV into harmony with the best scholarship of the seventies and eighties.

The program was, therefore, this: to update grammatical forms, to eliminate sex-biased vocabulary, and to incorporate the results of sound biblical scholarship into the translation.

The schedule of the meetings was always the same. On a Sunday night the members would arrive in Oberlin (later Princeton) and have dinner together; then, Monday morning, promptly at nine o'clock, the chair would call the whole group together for a general meeting, beginning with a Bible reading and a prayer, to receive communications, to consider matters of general policy, and to address specific issues that had arisen since the previous meeting. A representative from the Division of Education and Ministry of the NCCC was always present to express its continuing interest in, and support for, the committee's work; the representative usually sat in with one of the working groups for the rest of the day, to observe what was being done. In view of the size of the agenda to be covered in any week, these general meetings were kept as brief as possible. At the conclusion of the business meeting, the committee broke into subgroups for the Old Testament and New Testament. Later, as pressures to complete the job began to mount, the Old Testament committee was broken up into two, and finally three, subgroups. Eventually a subcommittee on the Apocrypha was added. Because this committee drew upon members from both Old Testa-

ment and New Testament, it usually met independently at
a different time of year

The sessions were exhausting for all the participants,
who, though unpaid, were without exception deeply, often
emotionally, concerned with every detail of the work being
done and therefore constantly on the *qui vive*. Since the
meetings lasted from 9 A.M. to 9 P.M., everyone was
thoroughly worn-out by the end of the week. Of course
there were breaks: there was a lunch hour from 12 to 2
(later, after a heartfelt plea from one exhausted scholar,
2:30!) and a dinner hour from 5 to 7 P.M. A fifteen-minute
break was allowed at the halfway point of the morning
and afternoon sessions, but for all practical purposes every
day involved eight hours of concentrated intellectual work.
It is a tribute to the character of the members that, in spite
of the pressures everyone felt, the sessions were generally
good-tempered — episodes marked by anger or irritation
were exceedingly rare.

III

The membership of the committee was structured so as to
be as representative as possible. The NRSV was intended to
be an ecumenical project. This would not have been
possible in the climate of the thirties, forties, and fifties
when the original RSV was planned and produced; with the
exception of one Jewish member, who was invited to join
the Old Testament section only at a rather late stage (and
is the only survivor of the original RSV committee to continue active on the NRSV), the old committee seems to have
been resolutely mainline Protestant in affiliation. But the

acceptance of the RSV by Roman Catholics in England, culminating in the publication of an official Catholic edition in 1966 in which the books of the Old Testament were arranged in the traditional Catholic order, supplemented by the Deuterocanonical books, opened the doors to genuine ecumenical collaboration. In 1973, the Collins Press of Glasgow issued an edition of the RSV entitled *The Common Bible,* in which the apocryphal books were placed between the Old Testament and New Testament, whereas the normal RSV order treated them as a supplement to the New Testament; and the Catholic Deuterocanonical books were distinguished, and printed separately, from the three additional books included in the standard Protestant collection of Apocrypha. In 1977 an expanded edition of *The Oxford Annotated Bible,* a study edition of the RSV, added 3 and 4 Maccabees and Psalm 151 to the Apocrypha, three items that belong to the liturgical tradition of the Eastern Orthodox Church. This last step made possible an edition of the NRSV that would be fully ecumenical both in content and preparation.

In accordance with the ecumenical perspective of the planning for the NRSV, the membership of the committee had been expanded to include Roman Catholic scholars, and the number of these tended to increase as the years passed, since they represented the largest single group of Christians in America. Moreover, the Roman Catholic Church, as an aspect of its revival of biblical studies generally, has produced a remarkable number of scholars of first-class ability. The Eastern tradition was represented by a leading scholar of the Greek Orthodox Church who served on both the New Testament and Apocrypha subcommittees. While, for obvious reasons, the Jewish community could not be expected to endorse any part of the

NRSV, the presence of an eminent Jewish scholar on the Old Testament committee, participating as a full contributing member, was intended as both an expression of goodwill and an assurance that the NRSV translation of the Hebrew Scriptures (the Christian Old Testament) would contain nothing offensive to our Jewish neighbors.

If, at the beginning, the NRSV committee was almost exclusively dominated by men (though there was one well-known woman scholar on the New Testament committee from the very start), this was not because the chair was indifferent to the situation, but rather because the relative scarcity of women scholars made it difficult for some of those invited to join to accept the committee's invitation. Nevertheless, as time went on, the number of women members and their contributions became substantial.

Each of the subgroups into which the Old Testament section was divided had its own presiding officer, at first the two vice-chairs; then, as the number of subgroups expanded to three, their ranks were increased by a chair pro tem chosen from within the new group. Each Old Testament subgroup was assigned a graduate-student secretary who was responsible for keeping track of the issues discussed and the decisions reached. Inasmuch as the conduct of the discussions was very informal, the secretaries were generally encouraged to take part in them when they felt impelled to do so. Obviously, they had the longest working day of all, since much of their labor took place after-hours.

The life of the committee naturally had a less serious side in the brief intervals between working sessions. Most of the members, like myself, looked forward to the opportunities presented by coffee breaks and mealtimes to talk with friends and engage in lively discussions with people of similar interests. Arguments begun in working sessions were often continued over meals; inevitably, one must admit, conversations were concerned with matters irrelevant to the matters in hand: sports, politics, travel, cultural activities, even gossip (!). After the nine o'clock adjournment there was still time for conviviality at a local restaurant or a visit to the last show at a local movie house. One of the inconveniences of the meetings at Oberlin was the limited opportunity for that kind of relaxation. The one year that Herbert May attempted to speed things up by having the committee meet for two successive weeks was never repeated, due to the energetic protests of one or two members who felt that two weeks in a town with only one picture show and practically no other opportunity for relaxing after work was one week too many.

IV

After Herbert May's tragic death in 1977, in an automobile accident, the general oversight of the committee devolved on Bruce M. Metzger, Professor of New Testament at Princeton Theological Seminary, who had previously served as chair only of the New Testament section. With his accession to the chair of the general committee, the venue of the meetings naturally shifted to Princeton, New Jersey, where it remained until the completion of the work, a period of about ten years. The sessions were housed at the seminary's Center of Continuing Education, where the members had their living quarters, and in the seminar rooms of the school's library just across the street. This was a happy arrangement since the library shelves were able to provide an answer to almost any question, however recondite, that might arise during the course of deliberations.

The procedure for dealing with the separate books of the Bible was very simple. At least one member in each group was assigned a particular book for study, and for as much research as necessary. When the member's study was finished, he or she then drew up a detailed list of all the changes he or she felt were either necessary or desirable. These agendas were then discussed *seriatim,* each item being either accepted immediately (as many were, of course, being in accordance with previous decisions) or discussed until a consensus was reached. In rare instances, discussion of a single item could go on for an hour or two. If, finally, no consensus seemed possible, the issue was decided by simple majority vote. At the end of the week all the changes voted by all of the subcommittees, after further discussion when it seemed necessary, were ratified at a general meeting. Since the committee's work went on for some fifteen years, with many changes in personnel, a large number of the Old Testament books were reviewed a second time by another subcommittee, following an agenda prepared by yet another scholar, since in the course of time the committee's understanding of its task had changed and matured; new general rules were formulated and the whole process of revision had become more thoroughgoing (some might say more radical) than had originally been envisaged.

The final stage in the process came when the work of the subcommittees was complete and the last book had been reviewed and re-reviewed. At this point the general committee voted to suspend operations and to elect an editorial committee consisting of five persons: Professor

Metzger, as chair both of the general committee and the New Testament section; two representatives from the New Testament subcommittee; and the two vice-chairs, both of whom represented the work on the Old Testament and the Apocrypha. Necessarily the two subcommittees (New Testament and Old Testament) met separately, with Professor Metzger presiding at each. This editorial committee was given power to determine the final form of the text before publication. The Old Testament and New Testament subcommittees met for sessions lasting a week or ten days, frequently at two-month intervals, and made a final review of every verse and almost every punctuation mark in the entire Bible, looking for inconsistencies in general style and the rendering of individual words, endeavoring to pull the whole together so that the NRSV would seem a unified work, not simply a collection of discrete translations.

The editorial committee was able to give thought to some matters, not strictly academic, that were of necessity largely passed over in the general committee, where pure scholarship tended to hold the floor. Inasmuch as the NRSV is sponsored by the National Council of Churches, it is intended for use in the services of the churches as well as for the private reading, study, and spiritual instruction of their members. For this reason attention needed to be given to the rhythm of sentences and the sound of words as they would be heard in public worship, and the general appropriateness of the text for a liturgical setting. Finally, since the NRSV was intended to be a revision of the RSV, not a new translation, it was important that it maintain, as far as is possible in modern English, the mood, tone, style, and uniform dignity of the KJV, which was the *original* Standard Bible.

As described above, the work of the subcommittees

covered three general areas. First was the comparatively simple procedure of removing "thee," "thou," and the corresponding archaic verb forms. Generally speaking, this was the easiest task. Occasionally, however, some further adjustment had to be made. One insignificant example occurs in the Lord's Prayer: "Our Father who art in heaven," mechanically corrected to modern style, would produce "Our Father who are in heaven," which, though a legitimate transformation at the mechanical level, would *sound* wrong to contemporary ears. Therefore the NRSV, like all other modern versions, simply omits the verbal copula and reads, "Our Father in heaven." It is true that this ignores one element in the Greek, the article, and has a more clipped, less resonant sound than the KJV, but such choices have to be made!

The second area to which attention had to be directed was insuring that the language was properly inclusive, so that no words intended by the original writer to refer to all human beings were translated by English words that might be understood to refer only to members of a single sex. The solution to these problems, which, in view of the peculiar nature of English, were often extremely difficult, was very time-consuming, since the resulting text had to sound like normal English, not some modish jargon. In only a tiny minimum of instances was the problem to prove insoluble — to us, at least. Two or three members of the committee, representing both the Old Testament and New Testament sections, resigned with the complaint that an inordinate amount of time was being spent on matters that seemed to them essentially trivial rather than on issues of substantial scholarly concern. The majority of the members, however, felt that the whole question was sufficiently important to warrant the time and effort spent upon it.

Since another chapter in this book deals with the subject at length, no more need be said about it here.

V

By far the most important discussions centered not on more or less routine items like the removal of archaic language forms or the introduction of inclusive language, but on substantive matters that concerned the meaning of the original Hebrew, Aramaic, or Greek and how this meaning is best expressed in modern literary English. In many cases the problem is the definition of a single word such as the Hebrew *ruach* or the Greek *pneuma,* either of which means both "wind" and "spirit." In the majority of instances the context makes the meaning clear, but in some passages such as Genesis 1:2 the context is completely neutral. Should one read with the King James Version "the Spirit of God," or, with most modern versions, something like "a divine wind" or "a mighty wind," since no creative function is ascribed to the *ruach* and its presence seems merely an accompanying circumstance? The reading of the NRSV, after much discussion, is "a wind from God," which is the same as that of the New Jewish Version. No member of the committee would feel assured that this translation is definitive, but it seems at least closer to the probable sense of the original Hebrew than the traditional rendering found in KJV and RSV. (RSV, it should be noted, offered a similar meaning in a footnote.)

One item that could almost stand as a paradigm of the kind of problem of which we are speaking, although a much simpler one than the meaning of *ruach* in Genesis

1:2, is the word "blessed" that occurs in a well-known "wisdom" formula found in both the Old Testament and New Testament. In the "Good News Bible" (Today's English Version), these words are rendered uniformly "happy," as can be seen in Psalm 1:1 and Matthew 5:3-11, and some would argue that this is a more accurate translation everywhere, especially since neither the Hebrew nor the Greek word is derived from the verb "to bless." Even the KJV and RSV sometimes render the Greek word by "happy" (for example, Rom 14:22, 1 Cor 7:40). But lexicographers argue that the Greek word *makarios,* in the classical form of the language, is used for that special happiness possessed by the gods and other divine beings, while a different word *(eudaimon)* describes the happiness enjoyed by ordinary human beings. The New Testament committee, in common with the translators of most other modern versions, opted to retain the word "blessed" in the Beatitudes and most other places. But the situation in Hebrew is altogether different in that the word *ashre* (actually a plural construct), which is translated "blessed" in KJV and RSV, is a form of the ordinary word for human happiness. So the Old Testament committee voted to change "blessed" to "happy" wherever it translates *ashre.* (The word "blessed" as applied to God is an altogether different matter and translates quite different Hebrew and Greek words. In such passages as Psalm 144:1, for example, NRSV, like all other versions, still reads "blessed." Rarely, the Hebrew word — *baruch* — is also applied to human beings, as, for example, in Ps 118:26.)

A word that raises very difficult problems in translating the New Testament is the Greek *doulos,* which the classical Greek lexicon defines unequivocally as "slave, bondman." Nevertheless, the KJV translated it 118 times as "servant": thus in Luke 2:29, "Lord, now lettest thou thy servant depart . . . ," a reading preserved verbatim in RSV. Many scholars, including some members of the NRSV committee, have argued that it should invariably be translated "slave," since other Greek words were available for "servant" if that had been the meaning intended. The counterargument is that in Greco-Roman society slaves were often highly respected persons who could hold responsible positions in society, whereas in American society the connotations of the word are entirely negative, as indicated by the adjective "slavish," or such denigrating phrases as "wage slave" or "slave of passion." It is also true that in Old Testament Greek the word *doulos* can designate someone in high authority like Naaman of Syria (2 Kings 5:1; cf. v. 6) and is used in other contexts in an obviously weakened sense. There are obviously good arguments on both sides of this issue and the final judgment had to be given by majority vote, which favored the retention of "servant" in such crucial passages as Luke 2:29, but with a new footnote, "Gk *slave.*"

These are just a few illustrations of the kind of complex problems the committee had to confront and the necessity of extended discussion to solve them. In other instances the data were of an entirely different character. Occasionally, for example, Old Testament passages have been illuminated by archaeological discoveries. A notable instance is found in the RSV at Genesis 14:19, where KJV-ASV describe God as "*possessor* of heaven and earth," but the RSV-NRSV text says "*maker* of heaven and earth." The change was based upon the discovery that in the ancient Canaanite language, as shown by the clay tablets found at Ras Shamra in Syria, the word *qanah*, which normally means "possess," once also had the meaning "create" or "make." Just such a discovery provides also the reason for an NRSV change in the text of Exodus 15:2, Psalm 118:14, and Isaiah 12:2, where both KJV and RSV read "The LORD is my strength and (my) *song*," a striking but rather unlikely coupling of ideas. It is now known, however, from inscriptions in ancient South Arabic (a dialect cognate with biblical Hebrew) that *zimrah,* which in biblical Hebrew usually means "song," could also mean something like "might" or "power." Furthermore, in the Septuagint, the ancient Greek translation of the Old Testament, the Exodus passage reads "my protector," which seems to point in the same direction. So in the NRSV, as in several other contemporary versions such as the New Jewish Bible, the line reads "The LORD is my strength and my *might*."

VI

Most of the changes made are not the result of new discoveries or scholarly insights, but rather the application of common sense. For example, it is surprising to note in a concordance to the KJV or RSV that the word "city" appears about seven times more frequently than the word "town." But it is obvious to anyone who has visited the country, or even thinks of the probabilities, that a very large proportion of these so-called cities are what we should call towns; Hebrew has words for "village" and "city," but no appropriate designation for the intermediate-sized "town." So the committee felt free to interpret the word "city" in accordance with what is known historically about the particular site. The Palestinian landscape, in consequence, is considerably less crowded with large municipalities in the

NRSV than in the older versions. Again, for the sake of greater accuracy, the "brook" Zered of Deuteronomy 2:13, which is actually a canyon nearly 4,000 feet deep at its lower end, and is some three to four miles wide, in the NRSV has now become the "Wadi" Zered, and the word "wadi" has been introduced in numerous other places where it is clearly the exact word required. The conjunction "lest" has been largely, if not entirely, eliminated from the NRSV vocabulary because some of us have discovered that even among college graduates many no longer understand its function. RSV Exodus 20:19, "let not God speak to us, lest we die" becomes in the NRSV, "do not let God speak to us, or we will die." In the KJV the word "animal" never appears; the only word used is "beast." The RSV slightly modernized by using "animal" in a few places, mostly having to do with laws concerning ritual purity. In the NRSV the situation is reversed and "animal" becomes the norm; "the beasts of the field" are now usually "the wild animals."

    None of the changes made, I think, was made just for the sake of being modern, but rather for the sake of greater clarity and accuracy. The fact that the discussion in this chapter has been necessarily concentrated on examples of things that have been changed may suggest to the reader that the revision is much more sweeping than is in fact the case. Much of the older text remains basically the same. One would hope that the changes that have been made would commend themselves to all readers as reasonable and necessary. But such universal agreement is not likely. The members of the committee recognize that no work of this kind can be regarded as final or definitive. A later generation may feel that still further revision is necessary in the light of increasing knowledge and the changing mores and language-style of human society. But the committee has worked long and devotedly and hopes that, at the very least, the NRSV is not unworthy to stand in the great succession headed by the KJV and continued in the RSV.

— II —

Recent Discoveries
and Bible Translation

WALTER HARRELSON

THE 1990s probably will not match the prior four decades in the production of new or revised English-language Bible translations. One of the reasons is that new discoveries of the magnitude of the Dead Sea Scrolls surely cannot be anticipated during the 1990s — although of course in the 1940s no one expected that a discovery of such magnitude was about to generate the fresh impetus to textual studies that followed in the wake of the scrolls' disclosure.

The scrolls contained copies or fragments of all of the books of the Hebrew Bible except Esther and of many of the Apocrypha, along with numbers of documents that belonged to the Jewish sect that produced the scrolls — probably the Essenes. The manuscripts date to the period 150 B.C. to A.D. 74 and are therefore a thousand or more years older than our earliest major manuscripts of the Hebrew Bible. On the whole, the scrolls agree closely with the later Hebrew manuscripts.

The scrolls have contributed immensely to textual studies and therefore to the work of Bible translators, whose fundamental job is to translate into the target language the best available Hebrew, Aramaic, Greek, or Latin text of the books of the Bible and the Apocrypha. There are several ways in which the scrolls have advanced this work. First, and most important, they have provided fresh readings of difficult texts in the Hebrew Bible, so that scholars are now often in the position of saying that one or more of the Dead Sea Scroll manuscripts of the biblical book in question either differs from or agrees with the Septuagint (the Greek Old Testament) or with some other early translation, against the Masoretic text. The Masoretic text is the standard Hebrew text produced by Jewish scholars over many centuries. The work on the text began as early as A.D. 500 or perhaps even earlier, and the Masoretic text was finally standardized by about A.D. 800.

Second, the Dead Sea Scrolls have offered additional or different meanings of biblical words and phrases, thereby enriching the lexical study of the biblical literature and contributing to the refining and recasting of many biblical verses or phrases, including some very well-known and treasured ones. Third, the scrolls have stimulated an enormous increase in the textual and lexical study of the Bible, with the result that exegetical study of the Scriptures, which of course goes on all the time, has recently been particularly fruitful in offering fresh understandings to contemporary Bible translators. Much of this exegetical study has not directly involved the materials found at Qumran (the site of the discovery of the scrolls, in the hills above the northwest corner of the Dead Sea). But none would deny that the spate of textual, literary, historical, and sociological studies of the Bible owes much to the discovery and study of the scrolls.

Our examination of the importance of recent discoveries for Bible translation must therefore distinguish those discoveries, like the scrolls, that have given us direct support for alternative readings of biblical passages from those discoveries that have contributed additional insight into the meanings of words and phrases, of customs and objects, and especially of legal and religious practices. The Dead Sea Scrolls have made the greatest contribution to the former, but all kinds of discoveries have contributed immensely to the latter.

I. DISCOVERIES LEADING DIRECTLY TO CHANGES IN TRANSLATION

A. 1 Samuel 10

One of the largest and most interesting changes in the biblical text lying behind the NRSV occurs at the end of 1 Samuel 10. For decades, scholars have pointed out that chapter 11 begins rather abruptly with the introduction of the hostility of Nahash the Ammonite against the citizens of Jabesh-gilead. Nahash agrees to spare its inhabitants if the males will submit to having their right eye gouged out. The Dead Sea Scrolls yielded fragments of three very important manuscripts of the books of Samuel. These fragments have not yet appeared in their definitive edition, but Professor Frank Cross of Harvard has readily made their contents available to scholars working on the books of Samuel. One of these manuscripts has a considerably larger text for the end of 1 Samuel 10 or, one could just as easily say, for the beginning of 1 Samuel 11. The Dead Sea

Samuel manuscript (identified in the note of the NRSV with the designation "Q ms") reads as follows:

> Now Nahash, king of the Ammonites, had been grievously oppressing the Gadites and the Reubenites. He would gouge out the right eye of each of them and would not grant Israel a deliverer. No one was left of the Israelites across the Jordan whose right eye Nahash, king of the Ammonites, had not gouged out. But there were seven thousand men who had escaped from the Ammonites and had entered Jabesh-gilead.

It is certainly possible that the Dead Sea Samuel manuscript supplied this additional material in order better to account for Nahash's demanding the right eye of the inhabitants. The first-century Jewish historian Josephus has a text quite close to the scrolls text, and Josephus is known to have smoothed out the biblical text from time to time. But the reading does not have the character of such an explanatory addition to an originally obscure text. It speaks of the Reubenites and the Gadites who had been plagued by Nahash in times past, describes the flight of 7,000 fugitives to Jabesh-gilead for safety, where they are then besieged "about a month later" (as the scrolls manuscript reads at 11:1). These fugitives in Jabesh-gilead agree finally to submit to the same maiming that Nahash had perpetrated on their colleagues, in the event that no champion could be found to come to their aid within the specified period. The NRSV translators had no difficulty in agreeing that this scrolls material belonged in the translation of the book of 1 Samuel.

The translators did have difficulty, however, in deciding how to designate these added sentences. The decision to place them as a separate paragraph at the end of chapter 10 was reached fairly easily; otherwise, we would have a large textual addition right at the beginning of chapter 11. But should they be numbered serially, following verse 27 of 1 Samuel? That was the original decision, and as a result five verses were included in the text of 1 Samuel that had never been in an English Bible to that time. But the more cautious decision was taken later on to include the material as a continuation of verse 27, for the sensible reason that readers could be puzzled if they found five verses in the NRSV that appeared in no other Bible.

B. 1 Samuel 1:11

Another interesting addition to the Masoretic text of 1 Samuel occurs in the first chapter, in the vow that Hannah is reported to have made at Shiloh. The Masoretic reading is, "She made a vow and said, 'O LORD of hosts, if only you will look on the misery of your servant, and remember me, and not forget your servant, but will give to your servant a male child, then I will give him to the LORD all the days of his life, and no razor shall touch his head.'" But fragments of one of the scrolls at 1:22 plus the Greek translation make it evident that the best text here, beginning after "male child," is "then I will set him before you as a nazirite until the day of his death. He shall drink neither wine nor intoxicants, and no razor shall touch his head." The support lent by the fragmentary text of the Qumran manuscript led the NRSV translators to accept this more probable reading into the text of 1 Samuel 1:11 and 1:22.

C. 1 Samuel 2:8

The scrolls manuscript supports the Greek in placing an additional line into verse 8 of Hannah's Song, but the NRSV translators decided not to accept that line. Verse 8 in NRSV reads:

> He raises up the poor from the dust;
>   he lifts the needy from the ash heap,
> to make them sit with princes
>   and inherit a seat of honor.

The additional line that was not accepted into NRSV reads:

> He grants the vow of the one who vows,
>   and blesses the years of the just.

The verse certainly fits into the poem excellently, but the translators finally decided, despite the support of the scrolls, that the Masoretic text is in this instance the more reliable. The additional line is given in a note rather than incorporated into the text of the poem.

D. 2 Samuel 22:36

The RSV translates 2 Samuel 22:36 as follows:

> Thou hast given me the shield of thy salvation,
>   and thy help made me great.

The last line reads the same in RSV's translation of the parallel to this ancient poem presented as Psalm 18 (Ps 18:35). The word in question is "help." RSV has a note indicating that the word might be translated as "gentle-ness," while the Masoretic text reads "your answering." The Hebrew word requires only the change of one letter to read what the RSV has translated — "help" — and the scrolls manuscript supports this reading. NRSV, accord-ingly, translates:

> You have given me the shield of your salvation,
>   and your help has made me great.

The word "help" has a note pointing out that the scrolls manuscript has this reading, while the Masoretic text reads "your answering," not "help."

E. 2 Samuel 23:1

A fascinating problem is presented by the opening line of David's so-called "Last Words" in 2 Samuel 23:1-7.[1] The Masoretic text has:

> The oracle of David, son of Jesse,
>   the oracle of the man who was raised on high.

But scholars had noted long ago that the Hebrew term translated "on high" (Hebrew *'al*) could be the name of a deity. Some had in fact translated ". . . whom El [or Al] exalted." But the Qumran manuscript that preserves parts of the end of 2 Samuel has the basic name of the West

---

1. See my essay entitled "Creative Spirit in the Old Testament: A Study of the Last Words of David (2 Samuel 23:1-7)," in *Sin, Salvation, and the Spirit,* ed. Daniel Duirken, O.S.B., 127-33. Collegeville, Minn.: The Liturgical Press, 1979.

Semitic deity El (Hebrew *'el*). Thus, there is no reason to
resort to the use of the alternate name of the deity or to
follow the Masoretic reading; the scrolls text yields the
meaning given in the NRSV, ". . . whom God exalted."

*   *   *

Studies of the Dead Sea Scrolls temple scroll and intensive
work on other cultic texts of the ancient Near East have
yielded a much better comprehension of the terminology
of the Israelite cult. A very large number of changes will
be evident as readers compare Leviticus in the RSV with
the NRSV rendering of the book. Let me mention only two
instances. First, throughout the Hebrew Bible the designation "peace offering" has become "offering of well-being,"
a term taken from the excellent translation of the Jewish
Publication Society, *Tanakh*. Second, the closing chapter of
Leviticus (chap. 27), dealing with votive offerings, has been
greatly modified to give clarity and precision to the detailed
list of payments that may be offered in lieu of animals or
grain to fulfill the terms of one's vows. The critical change
is to replace the vague RSV term "valuation" with the term
"equivalent," thus making it clear what this chapter is all
about.

II. DISCOVERIES AND FINDINGS RESULTING
FROM CONTINUING RESEARCH

Most of the changes in the NRSV result not from striking
new discoveries such as those mentioned above. They result
rather from the progress of biblical scholarship, frequently

arising from the further examination of discoveries made earlier, but often are simply the result of philological and exegetical scholarship that makes more precise the meaning of the biblical words or phrases or practices. Some of these are listed here, with brief comments.

A. Translations that give greater weight to the Masoretic tradition than does the RSV

The NRSV translators have been much less ready than the RSV translators to follow the Septuagint (LXX) against the Masoretic text. They have done so frequently, however, in books like 1 and 2 Samuel where the value of the LXX is unmistakable. Indeed, in general, the NRSV translators have given much more weight to Jewish tradition than their forebears, as the following illustrations will show.

1. Genesis 1:1   The question how to translate the opening sentence of the Hebrew Bible continues to be debated. It is evident from the openings of other creation stories in the ancient world, notably *Enuma Elish,* that a "when . . . then" pattern is customary. But the vocalization of the first word of the Bible, *Bereshith,* in the Masoretic tradition leads many scholars to believe that the nuance of meaning expressed by the first *two* biblical words, *Bereshith bara',* is best captured if both an absolute beginning and a temporal process can be conveyed by one's translation. For this reason, the NRSV has translated "In the beginning when God created the heavens and the earth . . . ," rather than "When God began to create. . . ." To translate, "In the beginning God created . . ." is to be too absolute (the Masoretes would have read *Bareshith* if that were their intention, it is believed), just as "When God began to create . . ." is too indefinite, although of course neither of those renderings is wrong or inadmissible. In fact, both alternatives are listed in the notes of NRSV.

2. Genesis 18:22   The Masoretes and other Jewish scholars preserved notices that at several points (traditionally eighteen of them) the text had been corrected in order to avoid misleading the reader or giving offense to God. These emendations (in Hebrew *Tiqqune sopherim*) have rarely been used to correct a biblical text, and NRSV rarely uses them to do so. But some of these are of such interest and value for a translation that they are included as notes to the text. That is the case with Genesis 18:22. The Masoretes report that the text originally read, "And the LORD continued to stand before Abraham." Such a reading, particularly in the context in which Abraham contends strongly with God for the city of Sodom, could be troublesome to readers, suggesting that God was subordinate to Abraham. The translation was therefore "corrected," according to tradition, to read as it now appears in the Hebrew text, "And Abraham continued to stand before the LORD." NRSV has a note reading, "Another ancient tradition reads, 'And the LORD continued to stand before Abraham.'"

3. Habakkuk 1:12   In Habakkuk 1:12 the NRSV now reads:

> Are you not from of old,
>   O LORD my God, my Holy One?
> You shall not die.

The translators have a note on the "You" stating that this is the reading of ancient Hebrew tradition, a reference to one of the scribal emendations. The note explains that the Masoretic text reads "We."

4. *Genesis 49:10*   A crux of biblical interpretation appears in Genesis 49:8-12, Jacob's blessing of his son (actually, of the tribe) Judah. The passage is probably speaking of some descendant of Judah (David is the historical personality in view, in all likelihood) who will rise to ascendancy over the tribes and bring rich blessing to all Israel. The expression ". . . until Shiloh comes" in verse 10 has long been a puzzle to translators and interpreters. The NRSV translators once again turned to early Jewish interpretations of such cruxes in the biblical literature. The Hebrew term translated "Shiloh" can be divided into two Hebrew words, the first *shay* and the second *loh,* with the meaning ". . . until tribute comes to him." Isaiah 18:7 has the word *shay* in a text promising that gifts will be brought to the Lord in a coming day from people now hostile to the Lord and to Israel. Our text may be speaking of the paying of tribute by the northern tribes to David during his seven-year reign in Hebron as king of Judah (see 2 Samuel 3).

5. *Job 32:3*   Another of the scribal corrections is reported to have occurred in Job 32:3. The introduction to the appearing of Elihu to challenge Job includes the statement that Elihu "was angry also at Job's three friends because they had found no answer, though they had declared Job to be in the wrong." But the Masoretes noted that the text originally had read, ". . . because they had found no an-

swer, and had put God in the wrong." This alternative is listed in a note to Job 32:3 in NRSV.

B. Translations resulting from continuing philological and exegetical work

1. Deuteronomy 33:27 One of the many biblical texts that has been subjected to intensive study through the decades is Deuteronomy 33, the Blessing of Moses. The familiar affirmation toward the close, in verse 27, "The eternal God is your dwelling place, and underneath are the everlasting arms," is a much beloved text. Contemporary study has revealed that such a translation is not as probable as that found in NRSV:

> He subdues [Hebrew participle from the verb *'anah*]
>   the ancient gods,
> shatters [Hebrew participle from the verb *ḥatat*] the
>   forces [literally "arms"] of old.

2. 2 Samuel 1:21 A similar revision of a difficult text has come about on the basis of numerous scholarly efforts. After the Ugaritic texts were discovered in northern Syria in the late 1920s, scholars began to pore over this collection of West Semitic literature, written in one of the oldest known alphabets, for parallels to biblical texts. The text in 2 Samuel 1:21 had long been a puzzle. What could it mean for David to lament over Saul and Jonathan by saying,

> You mountains of Gilbo'a
>   let there be no dew or rain upon you,
>   nor fields of offerings?

The last line clearly must have been wrong. Among the many proposed solutions, the RSV rendering was widely supported, ". . . nor upsurgings of the deep." But further study has concluded that the changing of the text to yield "the deep" is not really necessary. The text can be read, as in NRSV, ". . . nor bounteous fields," without any change in the Hebrew consonants. The curse / prayer of David, then, is that the place where Saul and Jonathan died in battle should remain unfertile forever, with no dew or rain falling upon it to provide bountiful harvests of grain.

3. *Isaiah 35:8*   The beautiful eschatological poem depicting the transformation of earth and of Zion found in Isaiah 35 presents a crux for translators in verse 8. The RSV renders this verse as follows:

> And a highway shall be there,
>   and it shall be called the Holy Way;
> the unclean shall not pass over it,
>   and fools shall not err therein.

The third line has a note indicating that the words ". . . and he is for them a wayfarer" appear in the Hebrew after ". . . pass over it."

Now, this translation seems to be altogether clear and adequate, until one recognizes that the exclusion of the "unclean" and the "fools" from the highway, and thus from the transformed Zion, is surprising when one observes that verses 3-6 are speaking about the weak and fearful, the blind, deaf, and speechless, who are to be prepared precisely to enter the transformed Zion. Thus it is hardly likely that the poet would, in verse 8, exclude the

unclean (perhaps the leprous in particular) and the fools
or simple ones.

The NRSV, in my judgment, does not adequately render the text but it does go some distance toward a correct
reading, especially in the footnote to "travel on it." NRSV
reads:

> A highway shall be there,
>   and it shall be called the Holy Way;
> the unclean shall not travel on it,
>   but it shall be for God's people;
>   no traveler, not even fools, shall go astray.

The NRSV has a note indicating that "travel on it" could
be read "pass it by." It also has a note on "God's people,"
mentioning that the Hebrew has "for them."

I would have preferred the following:

> A highway shall be there, a way;
>   it shall be called the Holy Way.
> The unclean shall not pass it by;
>   it shall be for them as well.
> Even fools shall not lose their way.

Such a reading gives cogency to this verse in light of the
earlier verses, showing that the eschatological poem is
speaking about God's preparing the wounded and damaged
and defective members of the community to find their place
in the transformed Zion, along with those more favored
by life.

4. Isaiah 63:8b-9 The striking reference to God's sharing
the distress and affliction of Israel in Isaiah 63:8b-9 has
disappeared in the NRSV. RSV reads:

. . . and he became their Savior.
In all their affliction he was afflicted,
    and the angel of his presence saved them.

The new translation, following the Old Latin and the Greek, translates a different vocalization for the Hebrew term *ṣr,* reading *ṣir* for the Masoretic vocalization *ṣar.* It then connects the last clause of verse 8 to the beginning of verse 9 and reads:

. . . and he became their savior
    [9] in all their distress.
It was no messenger [Hebrew *ṣir*] or angel
    but his presence that saved them.

Once again, a remarkable religious text is transformed as a result of the progress of exegesis. But two things should be kept in view. First, throughout the Bible there are texts that indicate God's sharing the suffering of the people, even if this text is eliminated. And second, this text is certainly remarkable as well: God not only sent intermediaries to bring deliverance to Israel but also it was God and no other, says the NRSV text, who intervened to save the people.

5. 2 Esdras 10:27 Another passage in which the fruits of exegesis have yielded an alternative reading with considerable importance is 2 Esdras 10:27. The change is in a single word. Two textual traditions exist, the Latin and the oriental versions. The latter are followed in RSV, which reads: "And I looked, and behold, the woman was no longer visible to me, but there was an established city, and a place of huge foundations showed itself." The context of the verse is Ezra's description of his fourth vision, in

which a grieving woman is suddenly transformed into
Zion. The question is whether the Zion being portrayed is
a fully established city that is miraculously revealed to Ezra,
or whether, with the Latin, we should rather read, ". . . but
there was a city being built," thereby indicating that the
massive foundations mentioned in the verse signify the
enormity of this Zion that is being prepared by God. NRSV
opts for this understanding, correctly, in my judgment. The
text from 2 Esdras then seems to build upon the vision of
Zechariah (2:1-5, in Hebrew 2:5-9), in which one angel
orders another to prevent the measuring of the dimensions
of Jerusalem. Jerusalem, it seems, is to be inhabited after
the manner of villages without walls. That is, it will grow
as necessary, in order to accommodate those whom *God*
brings to settle there. God and God alone will be its pro-
tecting wall.

Thus, much depends upon whether the reading should
be "established" or "being established." If the latter, as the
NRSV translators believe, then the openness of the future
and the human community's part in the fulfillment of the
divine purpose are underscored. That outlook would seem
to fit this portion of 2 Esdras better than the former, and
it would offer a kind of "solution" to Ezra's concern about
the fate of the wicked. The wicked, like the righteous, are
in the care of a just but also merciful God. And the prayers
of the faithful on behalf of the wicked, along with active
righteousness, may enable even the wicked to find a place
in the Zion that has no fixed boundaries.

C. *Changes of words or phrases*
in the interest of clarity or precision

Many of the changes in the NRSV have arisen in order to clarify given readings or to make them more precise. I will mention several of these, usually giving a biblical reference to one of the first of the changes made.

In Genesis 6:6, and frequently throughout the Hebrew Bible, the NRSV has changed the wording, "the LORD repented," to "the LORD was sorry," where it is clear that the reference is to the Deity's having rued a prior decision. When the emphasis falls on God's letting the divine anger subside, NRSV translates "relented," as in Amos 7:3. On other occasions, when it is clear that the point is that God's mind has changed, as in Exodus 32:12, NRSV translates "change your mind."

Genesis 13:2 mentions Abram's "cattle," according to the RSV, but here and often the NRSV reads "livestock," since the more inclusive word is certainly more appropriate. The Hebrew word *boqer* can include dairy cattle, bulls, and occasionally even sheep and goats.

In Genesis 34:31, NRSV has introduced the coarse term "whore" in order to express better the actual meaning of the passage. The same is done in other places, but the word is also frequently translated "prostitute."

In many places the Hebrew conjunction *ki* is translated as asseverative ("indeed") rather than as "for." An important instance occurs in Exodus 19:5: "Indeed, the whole earth is mine, but you shall be for me a priestly kingdom and a holy nation." Regularly, NRSV translates the RSV "children [or sons] of Israel" as "Israelites." The commandment against misuse of the divine name in Exodus 20:7 is translated, not as with RSV, "take the name

of the LORD your God in vain," but "make wrongful use
of the name of the LORD your God."

The ancient festivals have regularly been referred to
as "feasts" in English translations, thereby making it difficult to distinguish a real banquet from a religious festivity.
NRSV has regularly, but perhaps not always, substituted
"festival of Passover, Unleavened Bread, Weeks, Taber-
nacles," and the like.

One of the most difficult terms to translate was "ark
of the testimony" (Hebrew *'eduth;* see Exodus 26:34, for
example). This is a different term from the usual designation "ark of the covenant" (Hebrew *berith*), thus suggesting that some word other than "covenant" be found for
the different Hebrew term. But what English term is best?
The final decision of the translators was to use "covenant,"
but with a note indicating that "treaty" or "testimony"
would be an alternative reading, and also giving the Hebrew term in the note.

In the same Exodus verse occurs another special problem. The translation "mercy seat" for the Hebrew term
(kapporeth) has the support of centuries of familiar usage,
but is it accurate? On the other hand, simply to translate
"cover," because this object that sits upon the Ark of the
Covenant does provide a cover for it, seems inadequate to
express the actual import of this *kapporeth.* The Greek term
hilasterion means "that which produces expiation," or "a
gift intended to effect expiation." It was apparently Martin
Luther's translation "Gnadenstuhl" that led the King James
translators to produce "mercy seat." The NRSV translators
finally decided, in this case as well, to keep the customary
translation "mercy seat" but include a note reading: "or
cover." Both terms have some connection with the Hebrew
term, for that term seems to be related to the verbal root

kipper, "to make expiation" or "atonement." And, as noted above, the biblical text makes it clear that the *kapporeth* is in fact a cover, even if it is much more than a cover.

Some place names have been changed in order to avoid anachronisms. The designation "Syria" is not really accurate for biblical "Aram." When Syria comes into existence following the death of Alexander the Great (322 B.C.) the term is correct, and therefore it is used in references from that time. But the biblical term "Aram" should be rendered in just that way.

Ethiopia is a similar problem. Since, however, it is not clear just what African territory is being referred to in a particular biblical reference, the Hebrew term "Cush" has normally been translated "Ethiopia," with a note reading "or *Nubia;* Hebrew *Cush.*" The translators wished to make it clear that it often is not the territory now comprising modern Ethiopia that is referred to by the term "Cush," but more probably the territory lying to the immediate south of Egypt, along the Nile.

Geographical designations are also modified. The Hebrew *naḥal* is often translated "brook" in RSV; in NRSV it is more frequently translated "wadi," the term widely used today to designate a dry (or often dry) riverbed. NRSV therefore translates in 2 Kings 23:6 "the Wadi Kidron" for the valley to the east of Jerusalem. The general locality called "the entrance of Hamath" in Amos 6:14 and elsewhere becomes a specific locality: "Lebo-hamath," another of the fruits of exegesis and historical-geographical research.

The term for "city" in Hebrew often means what we today would call a "town." There are cities in ancient Israel, of course, but such expressions as 2 Kings 23:8, ". . . [Josiah] brought all the priests out of the cities of Judah . . . from Geba to Beersheba" are referring not just to the major cities, in all probability, but to both the cities and the smaller towns as well.

Sometimes, in fact, the term "daughters" (Hebrew *banoth*) means "towns," referring to the towns around a given city and probably connected with it administratively, and is so translated in NRSV (see Psalm 48:11, for example), but with a note indicating that the Hebrew has "daughters." In fact, it is occasionally difficult to be sure when the women of Jerusalem, for example, are being referred to and when the writer is speaking of the "daughter-towns" of Jerusalem. Another change affecting the expression "daughter of Jerusalem" is the decision to remove the word "of" and to translate "daughter Jerusalem" or "daughter Zion" (see Psalm 9:14, among many texts). The term "daughter" is a term of endearment and could be rendered, as some translators have done, "fair Jerusalem," "fair Zion."

The term "saints" occurs in RSV and in other versions as a translation for the Hebrew *hasidim,* but such a translation today is almost sure to mislead readers. Accordingly, "saints" has disappeared from the Old Testament of the NRSV in favor of the much more accurate "faithful ones," as in Psalm 116:15: "Precious in the sight of the LORD is the death of his faithful ones."

The effort to eliminate inappropriate or unnecessary masculine language also led the translators to recognize that some texts, when properly translated, give larger place to women than is evident in the present RSV translation. For example, Psalm 131:2 reads in RSV:

> But I have calmed and quieted my soul,
>   like a child quieted at its mother's breast;
>   like a child that is quieted is my soul.

The last line of this verse, however, is better rendered:

> like the weaned child that is upon me is my soul.

Since that translation suggests that it is the child's mother who speaks, earlier translators, including the King James translators, have simply not translated the Hebrew preposition "upon me." NRSV has rendered the line, "My soul is like the weaned child that is with me." Have we evidence that the psalm's author is a woman? It would appear so, though of course a male could have been holding the child.

The "sluggard" of Proverbs 6:6 and elsewhere becomes in NRSV "lazybones," and the "Preacher" of Ecclesiastes (1:1 and frequently) becomes the "Teacher." And in Song of Solomon 1:5, NRSV reads, "I am black and beautiful," not as in RSV, "I am very dark, but comely." No contrast is drawn linguistically between the young woman's blackness and her beauty, nor is verse 6 an acknowledgment that the dark skin color makes the speaker less attractive. The opposite may be intended by this verse.

Military and administrative terms have always been difficult to translate with confidence. One of these is the term translated "prince" in RSV and in other early English versions. While a number of Hebrew terms are rightly translated "prince," the Hebrew word *sar* most frequently does not have that meaning. In fact, it is never used in the Hebrew Bible for the son of a king, though it is used several times for persons of eminence and nobility — in which cases NRSV retains the translation "prince." In most instances, however, NRSV has settled upon "official" for this term. See, for example, Isaiah 1:23:

> Your officials [RSV "princes"] are rebels
> and companions of thieves. . . .

Another distinction made in NRSV that improves accuracy and precision of expression is that made between two Hebrew words translated in RSV by the one English word "Woe!" These two terms (in Hebrew *'oy* and *hoy*) do not mean the same thing. Hebrew *'oy* is the specific word for "Woe," a term used to express the pain, grief, and loss of one who cries out: "Woe is me," and the like. Hebrew *hoy*, however, means "Alas" or "Ah"; sometimes it is a sharp outcry to gain the immediate attention of hearers. In Isaiah 5:8, RSV translates too strongly: "Woe to you who join house to house and field to field." NRSV has simply,

> Ah, you who join house to house,
> and add field to field.

"Alas for you" would have served equally well. God is not pronouncing a curse at this point, but through the prophet is identifying the evil landsharks by the vivid description of their misdeeds. The true "Woe" comes in such texts as Isaiah 6:5: "Woe is me! I am lost."

Another Hebrew term difficult to translate is the word often rendered "evil" (Hebrew *ra'ah*) in such expressions as, "Does evil befall a city unless the LORD has done it?" (Amos 3:6 RSV). NRSV has some instances in which "evil" has been retained in such texts, but most of them have been changed. This word becomes "disaster" in NRSV (as in Amos 3:6); in other texts the translation is "calamity," or occasionally "punishment."

The term "flesh" often is used in the Bible to refer to the flesh of animals offered on the altar or used as a meal.

Occasionally it seems inappropriate to retain "flesh." In Ezekiel 24:10, for example, RSV reads, ". . . boil well the flesh. . . ." NRSV has "meat." There are also other instances of this kind.

Finally, it should be said that many other proposals for change in light of international exegetical and other studies have not been accepted by the NRSV translators. The new translation, like the RSV, is a translation in the tradition of the Authorized or King James Version. The translators were charged to make "necessary" changes, and they were therefore not at liberty simply to start over and do an entirely fresh translation. Thousands of changes were proposed that were not accepted, and in the final editing of the translation, some changes earlier accepted were modified to give greater consistency to the translation.

As a result, few if any of the translators are entirely satisfied with the final product. Even so, the purposes that were to be realized have, I believe, been realized. NRSV is an accurate translation that takes into account important discoveries of the past forty years. It has removed much of the "Hebrew English" that characterized the RSV, though not all of it, because that quality belongs to the King James tradition. And it has recast a very great deal of the language of the RSV that could be misleading in today's English. There are many excellent English translations of the Bible available today, and among them — perhaps it is right to say, chief among them — is the NRSV.

— III —

Problems Confronting
Translators of the Bible

BRUCE M. METZGER

IF, ACCORDING to the Proverbs of Solomon, "The way of the transgressor is hard" (Prov 13:15 KJV), the way of the translator is scarcely less so. Not only does the work of translating demand the utmost in concentrated effort, but the result will seldom please everyone — least of all the conscientious translator. Since not all the nuances in a text can be conveyed into another language, the translator must choose which ones are to be rendered and which are not. For this reason the cynic speaks of translation as "the art of making the right sacrifice," and the Italians have put the matter succinctly in a proverb, "The translator is a traitor" *(traduttore traditore)*. In short, except on a purely practical level, translation is never entirely successful. There is always what Ortega y Gasset called the misery and the splendor of the translation process.[1]

Now the work of translating the Bible presents special difficulties. Since the Scriptures are a source both of infor-

---

1. José Ortega y Gasset, *Obras completas,* vol. 5 (Madrid, 1983), pp. 427-55.

mation and inspiration, Bible translations are required to be accurate as well as felicitous. They must be suitable for rapid scanning as well as for detailed study, and suitable for ceremonial reading aloud to large and small audiences. Ideally, they should be intelligible and even inviting to readers of all ages, of all degrees of education, and of almost all degrees of intelligence.

Such an ideal is, of course, virtually impossible of realization. One can understand, therefore, why there have been so many attempts to put the Bible into English. Between 1952, when the Revised Standard Version was published, and 1989 twenty-six different translations of the entire Bible had been published in English, as well as twenty-five other English translations of the New Testament. In 1990, after seventeen years of work by the Standard Bible Committee of the National Council of Churches, the New Revised Standard Version was issued. It is the purpose of the present account to set forth some aspects of what Mgr. Ronald Knox aptly termed "trials of a translator."[2]

I. PROBLEMS CONFRONTING THE BIBLE TRANSLATOR

As background orientation, it will be appropriate to consider some of the kinds of problems that confront one who undertakes to produce a new translation of the Bible. In

---

2. This is the title given to the American printing (New York, 1949) of Knox's book issued in Britain under the title *On Englishing the Bible* (London, 1949).

addition to solving various kinds of textual, lexical, and literary problems, the translator must often face what can be called a psychological problem. This is the understandable reluctance on the part of some readers to accept a different rendering of the Scriptures from the one that they have been accustomed to read. To a degree not equaled with respect to other pieces of literature, Bible translators have sometimes had to face considerable hostility. An early example of such negative reactions to the faithful work of a translator was the experience of St. Jerome.

In the year 383 Pope Damasus commissioned Jerome to produce a uniform and dependable text of the Latin Bible; he was not to make a totally new version, but to revise the texts that were in circulation, using for this purpose the Hebrew and Greek originals. Jerome's first inclination was to say "No thank you" to the pope's invitation. He writes in his *Epistula ad Damasum,* which now stands in Latin manuscripts as a preface to Jerome's rendering of the Gospels:

> You urge me to revise the Old Latin version, and, as it were, to sit in judgment on the copies of the Scriptures that are now scattered throughout the world; and, inasmuch as they differ from one another, you would have me decide which of them agree with the Greek original. The labor is one of love, but at the same time it is both perilous and presumptuous — for in judging others I must be content to be judged by all. Is there anyone learned or unlearned, who, having taken the volume in hand and perceiving that what one reads does not suit the reader's settled tastes, will not break out immediately into violent language and call me a forger and a profane person for having had the audacity to add anything to the ancient books, or to make any changes or corrections therein?

There were two reasons, however, that prompted Jerome to incur such a degree of opprobrium. The first reason, as he goes on to say in his *Epistula,* was the command laid upon him by Damasus, the supreme pontiff. The second was the shocking diversity among the Old Latin manuscripts, there being, as he says, "almost as many forms of text as there are manuscripts" *(tot sunt [exemplaria] paene quot codices).*

Jerome's apprehension that he would be castigated for tampering with Holy Writ was not unfounded. His revision provoked both criticism and anger, sometimes with extraordinary vehemence. For his part, Jerome defended his work with forthright vigor, referring on occasion to his detractors as "two-legged asses" or "yelping dogs" — persons who "think that ignorance is equivalent to holiness." In the course of time, however, opposition to the revision subsided, and the superior accuracy and scholarship of Jerome's version came to be widely recognized. It was a clear case of the survival of the fittest.

In more modern times, the King James or so-called Authorized Version of the English Bible also met with a mixed reception at its publication in 1611. Dr. Hugh Broughton, a distinguished British scholar of both Hebrew and Greek, declared, "I had rather be rent in pieces by wild horses, than any such translation by my consent should be urged upon poor churches." In 1620 when the Pilgrims came to the New World, it appears that not one of them brought a copy of the 1611 Bible; it was too modern! They preferred the English Bible used by their grandparents, the Geneva version of 1560, the so-called Breeches Bible (from its rendering of Gen 3:7, "They sewed fig leaves together and made themselves breeches").

In our own century, when the Revised Standard Version of the Bible was issued in 1952, the new translation was vehemently castigated by those who were looking for an opportunity to calumniate the Federal Council of Churches, under whose auspices the new version had been produced. Unfounded and malicious accusations were brought against several members of the Bible Committee, to the effect that they were either communists or communist sympathizers — allegations that, at the insistence of Senator Joseph McCarthy of Wisconsin, were eventually printed, of all places, in the official United States Air Force Training Manual! Finally, after a thorough investigation conducted by nonpartisan authorities, this entirely unsupported charge was rebutted as "venomous nonsense" on the floor of the House of Representatives in Washington and the Manual in question was withdrawn.[3]

Meanwhile, the minister of a church in Rocky Mount, North Carolina, publicly burned with a blowtorch a copy of what he termed "a heretical, communist-inspired Bible." Thereafter he scooped up the ashes, put them in a tin box, and sent them to Dr. Luther Weigle, dean of Yale Divinity School, who had served as the chair of the Standard Bible translators. That box, with its contents, is now part of the books and archives of the Standard Bible Committee. Although in previous centuries Bible translators were sometimes burned, today happily only a copy of the translation meets such a fate!

Besides the perennial psychological problem that confronts translators and revisers of the Scriptures, the several kinds of recurring problems involving the translation

---

3. *The Congressional Record,* vol. 106, Part 3 (February 25, 1960), pp. 3505-07; Part 5 (March 29, 1960), pp. 6872-74; and Part 6 (April 19, 1960), pp. 8247-84.

process — textual, lexical, and literary — include the following.

(1) Obviously the first problem that faces the translator arises from the presence of differences in wording among the manuscripts of the Scriptures. These differences — some smaller, some larger — have arisen because, even with the best will in the world, a scribe copying a manuscript of some considerable length would almost inevitably make alterations in the wording. Furthermore, occasionally a scribe would deliberately introduce into the copy a slight change that seemed to be needed in order to clarify the meaning. For example, the older manuscripts of Mark 1:2-3 attribute to "the prophet Isaiah" the evangelist's quotations from both Malachi and Isaiah, whereas later manuscripts (followed by the King James translators in 1611) read "as it is written in the prophets" — an obvious amelioration of the earlier text.

By comparing the manuscript copies that survive, scholars seek to determine which reading best accounts for the rise of divergent readings. Bible translations differ because translators have differed in deciding which variant reading should be preferred as the original and which as secondary. In general, the wording of the older manuscripts can be trusted as likely to have suffered fewer scribal alterations than have recent manuscripts, since the latter are probably descendants of repeated stages of copying and recopying. Likewise the wording that makes a clarification of a difficulty in the text is generally to be regarded as a secondary reading. If such a reading has had wide circulation in the manuscripts, the translator may decide that it deserves to be made available to the reader. It is then placed in a footnote introduced by the statement, "Other ancient authorities read. . . ."

(2) After the translator has decided which form of the Hebrew or the Greek text should be taken as the basis of the English rendering, the second problem has to do with ascertaining the meaning of the words. Scholars are constantly attempting to learn more about the exact meaning of certain ancient Hebrew and Greek terms and expressions. The Hebrew Scriptures, for example, contain several hundred words and forms of words that occur in no other literature[4] and are therefore difficult to define. One such word is the word *pim,* which appears only in 1 Samuel 13:21. This word was taken by the translators of the King James Version to mean "a file," used by a blacksmith to sharpen hoes and other agricultural tools. During the twentieth century, however, archaeologists discovered in Palestine ancient sets of weights used for business transactions, each bearing a Hebrew word. One of these, weighing almost two and two-thirds ounces, is marked "pim" — and so translators now know that this was the amount the blacksmith charged for sharpening various tools.

In the Greek New Testament there are only a few such words (no more than two dozen) that occur in no other literature. One of them, however is an important word in the Lord's Prayer (Matt 6:9-13; Luke 11:2-4). In the petition, "Give us this day our *epiousion* bread," the adjective has been analyzed by lexicographers to mean either "daily" bread or bread "for tomorrow." In such cases, where a Hebrew or Greek word may legitimately be taken in two different ways, the translator should give the reader both renderings, placing one in the text and the other in a footnote. The latter will be preceded by the word "Or."

---

4. For a discussion of examples of such words, see Frederick E. Greenspahn, *Hapax Legomena in Biblical Hebrew* (Chico, 1984).

(3) Once the translator has decided which form of text to translate and what the Hebrew or Greek words mean, the problem of punctuation arises. In antiquity it was customary to write Hebrew and Greek manuscripts with few, if any, marks of punctuation. This means, therefore, that modern editors and translators must decide where a new sentence begins, where to insert commas, question marks, and other marks of punctuation. Naturally, opinions will sometimes differ. For example, the Lord's Prayer in the King James Version reads, "Thy will be done in earth, as it is in heaven" (Matt 6:10), whereas most modern versions punctuate it differently, "Thy will be done, on earth as in heaven." The principle that translators follow is to use the punctuation that gives the best and fullest sense. In this case the second way of punctuating is better, for it permits the phrase "on earth as in heaven" to be taken with all three preceding petitions, thus enlarging the scope and meaning of the prayer.

The beginning of a direct quotation can usually be determined without any trouble, it being indicated by some verb such as "said," "asked," "replied," or the like. But problems sometimes arise concerning the close of a quotation, for ancient scribes did not employ what we call quotation marks. Therefore, it is uncertain whether, for example, Jesus' reply to Nicodemus is intended to end at John 3:15 (RSV) or at 3:21 (NRSV).

(4) Another problem that confronts the translator is what to do with proper names that can also be used as common nouns. Should one transliterate the name or translate its meaning? For example, the Hebrew word *'adam* is a common noun meaning "a man" or "humanity" as well as a proper name. In the Book of Genesis the question soon arises at what point in the narrative one should begin to use

"Adam" rather than "the man." On this matter there is the widest range of disagreement among translators. Some versions make the change at Genesis 2:7 (the Targums), or at 2:16 (the Greek Septuagint), or at 2:19 (the KJV), or at 3:17 (RSV), or at 3:21 (New English Bible), or at 4:25 (NRSV). A similar problem in the New Testament concerns the Greek word *christos*, which can be transliterated "Christ" or translated either "anointed one" or "Messiah."

(5) During the past several years yet another problem has begun to confront the translator of the Bible. The question of the suitability of using male-oriented language in passages that obviously apply to both sexes has become a sensitive issue.[5] More and more people are coming to feel that it is inappropriate to use the word "man" or "men" when reference is being made to both men and women alike. Particularly problematic is the question how one can compensate for a deficiency in the English language, the absence of a common gender third person singular pronoun. In Matthew 18:2 the King James Version reads, "Jesus called a little child to him, and set him in the midst of them." Since, however, the Greek text does not indicate whether the child was a boy or a girl, is it legitimate to use the pronoun "him"?

Of course the several parts of the Bible arose in a patriarchal society that has left its imprint on the literary expression of the original text, and a faithful translator will not wish to falsify history by removing such indications. At the same time, however, the translator should be

---

5. For a balanced and insightful discussion of the problems confronting translators because of the inherent bias of the English language toward the masculine gender, see Paul Ellingworth, "Translating the Bible Inclusively," *Meta; Translators' Journal,* 32 (1987), 46-54.

careful not to introduce additional instances of masculine expressions where they are not present in the Hebrew and Greek texts. The King James Version more than once inserts the word "man" where it is lacking in the original. Examples include Revelation 3:20, "Behold, I stand at the door, and knock: if any man hear my voice, and open the door, I will come in." Here, instead of the word "man" is the Greek word meaning "anyone." The statement in Luke 17:34, "In that night there will be two in one bed," is a literal translation of the Greek, but the King James translators, abandoning this rendering found in all earlier English Bibles, saw fit to insert the word *men* so as to read "two *men* in one bed." The most egregious blunder of this kind appeared in the original 1611 rendering of Mark 10:18, where God was called a man: "There is no man good but one, that is, God." In printings of the King James Version after about 1645 this was changed to read, "There is none good but one, that is, God."

II. THE STANDARD BIBLE
COMMITTEE AND ITS WORK

The story of the New RSV Bible can be understood best if it is placed in historical perspective. It was in 1952 that the Standard Bible Committee finished preparing the Revised Standard Version of the Bible. This was a revision of the American Standard Version, published in 1901, which, in turn, embodied earlier revisions of the King James Version, published in 1611.

During the years following 1952 a number of important early manuscripts of the Gospels of Luke and John came to light (notably the Bodmer Greek Papyri), as well as increasing numbers of newly found Hebrew manuscripts from the Dead Sea area. Furthermore, continuing changes in the usage of the English language began to make some of the language used in the RSV sound archaic and stilted.

Consequently, in 1974 the Division of Education and Ministry of the National Council of Churches of Christ in the USA directed that the Standard Bible Committee[6] undertake a thorough revision of the RSV Bible, including the Apocrypha. Subsequently, in 1978, more precise directives were spelled out in terms of the following four mandates: necessary changes should be made (1) in paragraph structure and punctuation; (2) in the elimination of archaisms while retaining the flavor of the Tyndale – King James Bible tradition; (3) in striving for greater accuracy, clarity, and euphony; and (4) in eliminating masculine-oriented language relating to people, so far as this could be done without distorting passages that reflect the historical situation of ancient patriarchal culture and society. Within the constraints set by the original languages and by the mandates of the Division of Education, the committee followed the maxim, "As literal as possible, as free as necessary."

For the Old Testament the committee made use of the *Biblia Hebraica Stuttgartensia* (1977; ed. sec. emendata,

---

6. The Committee is composed of about thirty biblical scholars, representing ten different Protestant denominations. Among the thirty are also six Roman Catholic members, one Eastern Orthodox member, and one Jewish member, who worked with the Old Testament section. (For a list of the members, see Appendix.) The several members contributed their time and expertise, receiving no financial remuneration. Royalties on the sale of copies of the version are paid by the publishers to the National Council of Churches, supporting further work in the use and distribution of the Scriptures.

1983). For the Apocryphal/Deuterocanonical books of the Old Testament the committee made use of a number of texts (details can be found in the preface to the NRSV). For the New Testament the committee based its work on the most recent edition of *The Greek New Testament,* prepared by an interconfessional and international committee and published by the United Bible Societies.

In the course of discussing the several proposals, it is understandable that occasionally sharp differences of opinion would be expressed. What might seem to one person to be a matter of relatively minor importance might seem to another to be of major significance. Among the problems that confronted the committee in attempting to find the most appropriate rendering (or, in some cases, the least inappropriate rendering) were several that were debated more than once. One such question concerned the best way to translate the Hebrew word *miknas,* which refers to part of the high priest's linen garments. Traditionally this word has been rendered "breeches," but since the garment is said to extend from the loins to the thighs (Exod 28:42), that rendering seemed to be inappropriate. But what is more suitable? One of the older members said, "Why, of course, drawers is what is meant." Younger members proposed "shorts" or even "skivvies." Still others favored "pants" or "underpants." Eventually the somewhat cumbersome "undergarments" was chosen.

In the New Testament a recurring problem arose concerning the appropriate rendering of the Greek word *doulos.* Defined by classical Greek lexicons as "slave," this translation is certainly correct in many places in the New Testament, and a minority of the committee preferred this rendering everywhere in the NRSV. But other members were impressed by the fact that in the Septuagint *doulos* frequently renders the Hebrew word *'ebed,* a word variously translated "servant," "slave," "official," or "bondman." They were impressed also by the traditional rendering in English, German, French, Dutch, Spanish, and Italian versions in referring to Moses, David, and others in the Old Testament as the servant (not the slave) of God. Therefore, despite vigorous debates that were renewed more than once in the New Testament committee, the majority retained the traditional rendering of such passages as, "Paul, a servant of Jesus Christ" (Rom 1:1), "the song of Moses, the servant of God" (Rev 15:3), and "Praise our God, all you his servants" (Rev 19:5). In these passages a footnote now informs the reader that the Greek is literally *slave* or *slaves.*

Occasionally a change was voted that at a later session appeared to be ill-advised. Such was the proposal, adopted by the New Testament committee, that the Greek name *Ioudas* be always rendered throughout the New Testament by "Judas," including its occurrence in the title and verse 1 of the Letter of Jude. Here, however, further consideration convinced the majority that it would be better to follow current usage in English Bibles[7] and not, for reasons of linguistic purism, to introduce a rendering that would almost certainly have perplexed many readers. It was decided, therefore, that the best solution to this dilemma was to retain the traditional rendering in the Letter of Jude and to indicate in a footnote to verse 1 that the Greek reads *Judas.*

After the Old Testament and the New Testament sections of the RSV committee had completed their assign-

---

7. Earlier English translations of the Bible, such as those of Wycliffe (1380), Tyndale (1534), Coverdale (1535), and the Great Bible (1539), used Iudas or Judas. Moffatt (1913) used Judas in verse 1 and for the title printed "The Epistle of Judas (Jude)."

ments, the results were turned over to two editorial committees for necessary smoothing and standardizing of work that had extended over a span of fifteen years. During that time a certain dynamic had evolved, which meant that adjustments needed to be made in each Testament. This editorial work was accomplished for the Old Testament and the Apocryphal/Deuterocanonical books by Robert Dentan, Walter Harrelson, and Bruce Metzger, meeting for seventy-six days, and for the New Testament by Paul Minear, Lucetta Mowry, and Bruce Metzger, meeting for thirty-three days. Finally, it was the responsibility of the chair to introduce at the very end a number of adjustments within, and between, the two Testaments.

Near the close of the work of the entire committee, attention was given to the question of what to call the revision. In selecting a suitable designation for the updated form of the Revised Standard Version, two considerations needed to be balanced with each other: (1) the name ought to show some degree of continuity of the revision with the previous form of the version; (2) at the same time the name should be distinctive and not easily confused with other existing English versions.

In accordance with the former consideration it was thought necessary to retain "Revised Standard" (or at least the word "Standard") in the name. Possible designations, accordingly, were "Ecumenical Standard Version," and "New Standard Version." It was also suggested that "Revised Standard Version" be retained, followed by one of the following, "New Edition," or "1990 Edition," or "Final Edition."

Another possibility was to use "Revised Standard Version" with a prefix; among those that were considered were "New," "Second," and "Improved." Of course, one needs to take into account the acronym that would be formed

from the name given to the version — and the last mentioned possibility would have resulted in the IRS version!
Eventually the name that was approved as the most satisfactory was the New Revised Standard Version.

A word may be added about the format of the version.
The NRSV has half-title pages for the Old Testament, the
Apocryphal/Deuterocanonical Books (when they are included in an edition), and the New Testament. The original
title page of the 1946 RSV New Testament was adopted as
a half-title page:

The New Covenant

commonly called

THE NEW TESTAMENT
of our Lord and Savior Jesus Christ

For the Old Testament the following half-title page
was adopted:

The Hebrew Scriptures

commonly called

THE OLD TESTAMENT

In copies that contain the books of the Apocrypha
between the Old and New Testaments (a feature that *all*
copies of the King James Version used to have) the half-title
page reads:

THE APOCRYPHAL/
DEUTEROCANONICAL BOOKS
of the Old Testament

The books in this last section are placed in four groupings, in accordance with the differing usages of the several churches that accept some of the books as deuterocanonical.

(a) Books and parts of books that are in Roman Catholic, Greek, and Slavonic Bibles.

(b) Books in Greek and Slavonic Bibles, but not in the Roman Catholic canon.

(c) Books in the Slavonic Bible and in the Latin Vulgate Appendix.

(d) Books in an Appendix to the Greek Bible.

Such matters as the inclusion of section headings, cross-references, and clues to the pronunciation of proper names have been left to the discretion of the seven licensed publishers.[8] These are (in alphabetical order) the Cambridge University Press, Holman Bible Publishers, Thomas Nelson Publishers, Oxford University Press, World Bible Publishers, and the Zondervan Corporation. In Great Brit-

---

8. Also at the discretion of the publisher is the decision whether to use red ink in printing the words attributed to Jesus, a format begun in 1899 when Louis Klopsch prepared a New Testament issued by the Christian Herald press in New York. Members of the Standard Bible Committee have grave reservations about the propriety of issuing the Bible in such a format. Besides the difficulty of ascertaining which are the words of Jesus (see, for example, p. 54 above concerning the punctuation of John 3:15-21), such a procedure not only destroys the unity of the text of New Testament books but also implies a theological judgment that what Jesus said is more significant than what he did.

ain, besides the two university presses, the Glasgow publishers, William Collins Sons and Co., issue the NRSV.

III. EXAMPLES OF CHANGES ADOPTED FOR THE NEW REVISED STANDARD VERSION

The following examples, arranged in various categories, will disclose something of the literary character of the New Revised Standard Version.

Among the words that are not in the Revised Standard Version (1952), the New Revised Standard Version contains the following (the corresponding rendering of the RSV is given within parentheses):

attorney (spokesman) Acts 24:1

bungler (sinner) Eccl 9:18

chiseled (carved) 2 Cor 3:7

disciplinarian (custodian) Gal 3:24f.

encroach (draw near) Deut 2:37

exploited (grasped) Phil 2:6

fiancée (betrothed) 1 Cor 7:36-38

lazybones (sluggard) Prov 6:6 and 9

liberator (judge) Acts 7:35

litigation (judgment) Hos 10:4

loungers (those who stretch themselves) Am 6:7

mauled (tore) 2 Kings 2:24

nagged (pressed hard) Judg 14:17; 16:16

pestered (urged) Judg 16:16

rogues (unjust) Lk 18:11

ruffians (wicked fellows of the rabble) Acts 17:5

scoundrels (base fellows) Deut 13:13

spellbound (astonished) Mk 11:18

wadi (valley) Deut 2:27 etc.

A new proper name is provided in a footnote to the rendering "loyal companion" at Philippians 4:3, namely "Or *loyal Syzygus.*"

On the other hand, the following words that are present in the RSV were not kept in the NRSV: ass (except "wild asses"), dumb, fetch, girdle, hart, lest, scourge (verb), victuals. The two words "for ever" are now written as one word, and "none," when referring to a person, is written "no one." Instead of the rather haphazard use of "which" and "that" in most English Bibles, the committee, following the preference indicated by H. W. Fowler in his *Modern English Usage,* restricted the use of "which" to instances when it follows a comma or a preposition, and used "that" in most other cases. The expressions "you all" and "them all" are replaced by "all of you" and "all of them."

Among the phrases that might be regarded as typical of biblical English, the following among many that could be mentioned have been altered in the NRSV (the second of each pair is the NRSV wording):

burn incense/offer incense

David the king/King David

fine flour/choice flour

Jeremiah the prophet/the prophet Jeremiah

peace offering/offering of well-being

Significant changes in specific passages include the following. For convenience of comparison, the first text in each of the following pairs is that of the RSV (1952).

(1) Greater accuracy

Amos 6:5	. . . like David invent for themselves instruments of music.
NRSV	. . . like David improvise on instruments of music.
Luke 7:47	Her sins, which are many, are forgiven, for she loved much.
NRSV	Her sins, which were many, have been forgiven; hence she has shown great love.
John 2:15	Making a whip of cords, he drove them all, with the sheep and oxen, out of the temple.
NRSV	Making a whip of cords, he drove all of them out of the temple, both the sheep and the cattle.

(2) Improved clarity

Exodus 11:8	And he [Moses] went out from Pharaoh in hot anger.
NRSV	And in hot anger he left Pharaoh.
1 Samuel 11:2	. . . gouge out all your right eyes.
NRSV	. . . gouge out everyone's right eye.
Micah 1:11	The wailing of Beth-ezel shall take away from you its standing place.

NRSV   Beth-ezel is wailing, and shall remove its
                    support from you.

Zechariah 3:3   Now Joshua was standing before the
                    angel, clothed in filthy garments.
NRSV   Now Joshua was dressed in filthy clothes
                    as he stood before the angel.

(3) *More intelligible English*

Psalm 86:11   Unite my heart to fear thy name.
NRSV   Give me an undivided heart to revere
                    your name.

2 Corinthians   Our mouth is open to you, Corinthians;
  6:11   our heart is wide.
NRSV   We have spoken frankly to you Corinthi-
                    ans; our heart is open to you.

2 Corinthians   Open your hearts to us.
  7:2
NRSV   Make room in your hearts for us.

(4) *More natural English*

Deuteronomy   Your sandals have not worn off your feet.
  29:5
NSV   The sandals on your feet have not worn
                    out.

1 Samuel 24:11   Though you hunt my life to take it . . .

NRSV	Though you are hunting me to take my life . . .

Psalm 98:8	Let the hills sing for joy together.
NRSV	Let the hills sing together for joy.

Matthew 12:34	How can you speak good, when you are evil?
NRSV	How can you speak good things when you are evil?

Acts 12:6	The very night when Herod was about to bring him out, Peter was sleeping between two soldiers, bound with two chains . . .
NRSV	The very night before Herod was going to bring him out, Peter, bound with two chains, was sleeping between two soldiers . . .

Hebrews 11:16	God prepared for them a city.
NRSV	God prepared a city for them.

(5) Adjustment of renderings that could be misunderstood

1 Kings 19:21	Then he arose and went after Elijah.
NRSV	Then he set out and followed Elijah.

Psalm 39:8	I am dumb . . .
NRSV	I am silent . . .

| Psalm 50:9 | I will accept no bull from your house. |
| NRSV | I will not accept a bull from your house. |

| Psalm 119:86 | All thy commandments are sure; they persecute me with falsehood. |
| NRSV | All your commandments are enduring; I am persecuted without cause. |

| 2 Corinthians 11:25 | Once I was stoned. |
| NRSV | Once I received a stoning. |

(6) *Avoidance of ambiguity in oral reading*

| Genesis 35:7 | Because there God had revealed himself. |
| NRSV | Because it was there that God had revealed himself. |

| Psalm 122:5 | There thrones for judgment were set. |
| NRSV | For there the thrones for judgment were set. |

| Luke 22:35 | "Did you lack anything?" They said, "Nothing." |
| NRSV | "Did you lack anything?" They said, "No, not a thing." |

(7) *Better euphony*

| Isaiah 6:2 | With two he flew. |
| NRSV | With two they flew. |

Isaiah 22:16   You have hewn here a tomb for yourself,
                you who hew a tomb on the height.

NRSV   You have cut out a tomb for yourself,
                cutting a tomb on the height.

Luke 19:32   Those that were sent went.
NRSV   Those who were sent departed.

(8) Elimination of "man" or "men" when neither occurs in the original text

Matthew 6:30   O men of little faith.
NRSV   — you of little faith.

John 2:10   Every man serves the good wine first; and
                when men have drunk freely, then the
                poor wine.
NRSV   Everyone serves the good wine first, and
                then the inferior wine after the guests
                have become drunk.

John 12:32   And I, when I am lifted up from the
                earth, will draw all men to myself
NRSV   And I, when I am lifted up from the
                earth, will draw all people to myself.

Romans 16:7   They are men of note among the apos-
                tles.
NRSV   They are prominent among the apostles.

70   *Bruce M. Metzger*

(9) Elimination of unnecessary masculine renderings

Matthew 4:4	Man does not live by bread alone.
NRSV	One does not live by bread alone.

Luke 6:45	The good man out of the good treasure of his heart produces good, and the evil man out of the evil treasure produces evil.
NRSV	The good person out of the good treasure of the heart produces good, and the evil person out of the evil treasure produces evil.

Galatians 6:6	Let him who is taught the word share all good things with him who teaches.
NRSV	Those who are taught the word must share in all good things with their teacher.

2 Corinthians 10:17	Let him who boasts, boast of the Lord.
NRSV	Let the one who boasts, boast in the Lord.

Ephesians 3:16	Grant you to be strengthened with might through his Spirit in the inner man.
NRSV	Grant that you may be strengthened in your inner being with power through his Spirit.

Ephesians 4:28	Let the thief no longer steal, but rather

	let him labor, doing honest work with his hands.
NRSV	Thieves must give up stealing; rather let them labor and work honestly with their own hands.

Revelation 2:29	He who has an ear, let him hear what the Spirit says to the churches.
NRSV	Let anyone who has an ear listen to what the Spirit is saying to the churches.

N.B.	No changes have been made in language pertaining to the Deity.

CONCLUSION

No translation of the Scriptures is perfect, as anyone who has ever tried to make one will be ready to acknowledge. Luther, it is said, issued nineteen revisions of his German Bible. At the close of seventeen years of work on the NRSV, probably all members of the committee felt a mixture of relief and regret — relief that the work was finished, but also regret that still further "fine tuning" would have made a better rendering. In any case, there comes a time when one must say enough is enough. In the concluding words of the Preface to the NRSV, the committee speaks to the reader as follows:

We have resisted the temptation to introduce terms and phrases that merely reflect current moods, and have tried to put the message of the Scriptures in simple, enduring words and expressions that are worthy to stand in the great tradition of the King James Bible and its predecessors.

In traditional Judaism and Christianity, the Bible has been more than a historical document to be preserved or a classic of literature to be cherished and admired; it is recognized as the unique record of God's dealings with people over the ages. The Old Testament sets forth the call of a special people to enter into covenant relation with the God of justice and steadfast love and to bring God's law to the nations. The New Testament records the life and work of Jesus Christ, the one in whom "the Word became flesh," as well as describes the rise and spread of the early Christian Church. The Bible carries its full message, not to those who regard it simply as a noble literary heritage of the past or who wish to use it to enhance political purposes and advance otherwise desirable goals, but to all persons and communities who read it so that they may discern and understand what God is saying to them. That message must not be disguised in phrases that are no longer clear, or hidden under words that have changed or lost their meaning; it must be presented in language that is direct and plain and meaningful to people today. It is the hope and prayer of the translators that this version of the Bible may continue to hold a large place in congregational life and to speak to all readers, young and old alike, helping them to understand and believe and respond to its message.

— IV —

Inclusive Language in the New Revised Standard Version

WALTER HARRELSON

I. GETTING STARTED

THE COMMITTEE responsible for producing the NRSV did not begin with a mandate to make the language inclusive. The decision was taken along the way, and in stages, as the work of the committee proceeded. The first formal statement on the subject was a page produced by the late George MacRae, S.J., containing guidelines for avoiding masculine language in cases in which it was clear that both men and women were intended. It was a modest statement indeed and was soon outgrown, but it served us well for several sessions. We did not engage in extended discussion about avoiding masculine references to the Deity, although we reviewed the matter as the draft of the Inclusive Language Lectionary was being produced, at which time the translation committee reaffirmed its decision not to attempt to eliminate masculine references to God.

But as the work proceeded, several committee members were unhappy about two matters. First, we had only one woman member of the committee, a fact that continued to trouble us. The committtee had made efforts in the 1970s, and perhaps earlier, to secure the assent of women scholars to serve on the committee, but without success. On one occasion, probably around 1980, committee members at a business session of the entire committee proposed that we invite *several* women scholars at once and see if we could secure acceptances in that way. The plan succeeded, and several women scholars joined the committee during the next few years. Their presence gave additional incentive to the effort to eliminate more of the masculine language than our draft translations had done to that point, although not all of the women scholars held identical positions on this matter.

The second concern arose when it was perceived how extensively we were retaining masculine language in our draft translations. Could we eliminate more of it and still remain within our mandate to revise the RSV only where it was necessary to do so? What strategies were available that we might not yet have tried? The usual approach was taken: a small committee was appointed to take some particularly difficult texts and see what could be done to reduce or eliminate the masculine references. The texts chosen were Exodus 21 to 23, the so-called Covenant Code, and Joshua 20, one of the accounts concerning the establishment of cities of refuge. The committee did its work primarily by correspondence, with an exchange of drafts of the two passages. The proposed changes were not greatly different from what we now have in the NRSV, but when they were presented to the entire committee, it was clear that they were not acceptable at all. To eliminate the "his" in such legislation as "whoever strikes his father or his mother shall be put to death" (Exod 21:15) was considered too radical, and making the sentence plural clearly would not work. (Later, of course, we frequently introduced the plural.) And in any case, legal language, it was pointed out, is conventional, stereotyped language, well understood by the community to apply to all, but necessarily put in fixed, conventional terms. It would be bad precedent indeed to begin to modify the Bible's legal language in the manner proposed. What we needed was greater precision in the use of this stereotypical language, a precision that was being helped along by the many specialist studies of ancient Near Eastern and biblical law. We risked introducing only confusion when what was urgently needed was greater clarity.

The same was said about the revision of the text concerning cities of refuge. In this case the draft had proposed that we use "the slayer" and "the victim" as an alternate to using the pronoun "he" so often. It seemed to the drafters of the proposal that these changes made things much clearer, for they identified the parties much more precisely. But the time was not ripe for such a change, and the draft proposals were voted down. The full committee indicated its desire not to try to make the legal language of the Bible gender-inclusive, although I believe no formal vote to that effect was taken.

Thereafter, the several groups working on the Hebrew Bible, the Apocrypha, and the New Testament simply worked out their own approaches, sharing them over meals and in general discussion with other groups, and a consensus was built up over the remaining years that we could and must eliminate masculine language that was not clearly intended to refer only to males. A number of strategies were devised for doing so, and the result is reflected in the NRSV. The two small editorial committees that went through the entire text (one for the Hebrew Bible and the

Apocrypha and one for the New Testament) were charged to catch the remaining omissions that could be changed and to smooth out, to the extent possible, the varied practices of the several groups.

II. THE INCLUSIVE LANGUAGE POLICY

The policy that was developed over the last decade of the committee's life finally came to have the assent of all members. That policy was quite simple: the committee should remove all masculine language referring to human beings apart from texts that clearly referred to men. To achieve this the committee adopted a number of agreed conventions (chief among them the use of the plural instead of the singular) even in some instances in which the committee believed that only males were involved ("My child" for "My son" in Proverbs, for example). It was agreed that we would not use "persons" or "people," unless no alternative could be found. We would use "one" or "someone" as necessary, but sparingly. When a Psalmist was referring to an enemy, we sometimes would retain the "he" or "his" in order not to lose the vivid, personal force of the psalm. Certain critical texts, such as those that employed "son of man" for humankind, were at first handled on an ad hoc basis, but as the work proceeded those, too, began to be eliminated. Ezekiel's many references to the prophet as "son of man" (Hebrew *ben 'adam*) were translated "O mortal" or "mortal," a happy solution, we thought, since Ezekiel is clearly stressing the prophet's humanity in contrast to God's transcendent glory and authority.

Daniel's "son of man" was treated differently, since

there the Aramaic "one like a human being," which was
the translation adopted, clearly means just that. The New
Testament references, however, retain Son of Man, because
in the Gospels this term often functions as a title.

Have the translators been consistent in their application of the policy? They have been, on the whole, quite
successful, with the result that readers now have a largely
inclusive-language translation that can easily be made still
more inclusive even as one reads from the lectern or pulpit.
Let me illustrate and make some comments about particularly troublesome cases.

Psalm 8 is a good instance of the principle of making
texts inclusive by the use of the plural pronoun. I begin
with verse 3:

> When I look at your heavens, the work of your fingers,
>   the moon and the stars that you have established,
> what are human beings that you are mindful of them,
>   mortals that you care for them?
> Yet you have made them a little lower than God,
>   and crowned them with glory and honor . . .

It is unmistakable that these plurals express more clearly,
for contemporary English readers, the sense of the Hebrew
text than singular number pronouns would express that
sense. And in this instance the use of the plural for the
Hebrew terms *'enosh* and *ben 'adam* renders the meaning
just as well as "man" and "son of man," unless one is
interpreting the psalm to have reference to Israel's divinized
earthly king, as some scholars still do.

The problem of how to quote this text in Hebrews
2:6 is solved by simply using the terms for "man" and "son
of man" that had been used to translate the Hebrew text.
The Greek is given in footnotes, along with an additional

note to the effect that the terms "man" and "son of man" in the Hebrew text refer to all humankind. I wonder, today, if we could not have made that footnote more clear, since we do not in fact use "man" and "son of man" in the translation of the Hebrew psalm.

Another example of the committee's practice, involving more change, occurs in the translation of Psalm 41. There we decided to translate some direct speech as indirect speech in order to use inclusive language. Instead of translating, "My enemies say in malice, 'When will he [i.e., the Psalmist] die, and his name perish?'" we translate, "My enemies wonder in malice when I will die, and my name perish." And again, in verse 8, we have, "They think that a deadly thing has fastened on me, that I will not rise again from where I lie," for the direct quotation, "They say, 'A deadly thing has fastened on him; he will not rise again from where he lies.'" Such a change could be criticized for diminishing the concreteness and vividness of the Psalmist's language, but I believe that little has been lost in our rendering.

But we were not able to make all the language inclusive, nor were our colleagues who translated the New Testament. In the translation of Psalm 109, for example, we finally agreed that we would have to let some masculine references remain, since otherwise the Psalmist's enemy could not adequately be depicted in contrast to the Psalmist. Note verse 6, where we have introduced the words, "They say," in order to make it clear that it is the Psalmist's accuser who calls down the terrible curse on the Psalmist, not the other way around (vv. 7-19). The Psalmist's prayer resumes at verse 20, where the language is once more inclusive. But the Psalmist has been *necessarily* identified as male, though we could have translated, "They call for a wicked person to be appointed against me / for an accuser to stand on my right. / When I am tried, let me be found guilty . . . ," and so on — following the device used in Psalm 41.

The fact is that we tried that approach, but the farther we proceeded, the more complicated matters got. See, for example, verse 17: "I loved to curse, they said; let curses come on me." It was too much and too confusing, with the result that we gave up on Psalm 109 and left the Psalmist identified as masculine.

One happy discovery was that Psalm 131 is translated in such a way as to suggest that the author was a woman, not a man. See especially verse 2, which now reads at the end: ". . . my soul is like the weaned child that is with me." This is surely a precise translation of the Hebrew, and following upon the preceding line, ". . . like a weaned child with its mother . . . ," strongly suggests that a mother is speaking.

The New Testament committee evidently gave up on Matthew 5:25, where the text still reads, "Come to terms quickly with your accuser while you are on the way to court with him. . . ." I would, however, have preferred to read ". . . while the two of you are on the way to court. . . ."

III. INCLUSIVE LANGUAGE THAT WORKS PARTICULARLY WELL

I can also cite some instances of inclusive language that in my judgment the translators have handled particularly well. In the New Testament, I single out several instances

from 1 Corinthians and elsewhere that I think are praise-
worthy. Beginning at 1:10 and throughout the letter,
"brothers" has very often become "brothers and sisters,"
with a note that indicates that the Greek reads "brothers."
Other instances of "brothers" in the Greek need to be
translated otherwise. For example, in 1 Corinthians 14:26,
"my brothers" becomes "my friends," as it does also in
14:39. But in 6:6, "brother" and "brothers" have become
". . . a believer goes to court against a believer." The
changes for the sake of inclusiveness once again result in
a more satisfactory rendering than would a literalistic
translation of the normal meaning of the Greek.

In other places, both the New Testament and the Old
Testament committees have rendered "brother" by "neighbor" or "kin," a good solution in many instances, although
there are distinct Hebrew and Greek words for "neighbor,"
and readers could suppose, were there not a note, that the
Hebrew or Greek has the usual word for "neighbor."
Numerous instances of this kind of inclusive translation
occur. See, for example, Matthew 7:3, ". . . the speck in
your neighbor's eye," and Leviticus 19:17, "You shall not
hate in your heart anyone of your kin." When "kin" or
"kinsfolk" is chosen for "brother" or "brothers,"
frequently no note is given.

For "man" or "men," many different solutions are
found. In 1 Corinthians 1:25, NRSV reads, "For God's fool-
ishness is wiser than human wisdom, and God's weakness
is stronger than human strength." Genesis 9:6 reads,
"Whoever sheds the blood of a human, / by a human shall
that person's blood be shed; / for in his own image / God
made humankind." That limps quite a bit poetically,
though the committee trying to revise that little poem
worked hours on it — but at that point we had not quite

hit our stride in discovering inclusive language. The use of "others" is often a successful solution; see Matthew 6:1, "Beware of practicing your piety before others. . . ." We also frequently use "one" and "anyone."

In Acts 2 it would have been possible to treat 2:14 in the way that 2:22 is treated, reading the first passage "You that are Judeans" instead of "Men of Judea," just as 2:22 reads "You that are Israelites." Similarly, in Genesis 2:7, we could have read ". . . then the LORD God formed a man . . ." instead of "then the LORD God formed man." I fear that we may have overlooked a number of other passages where the text could have been made inclusive.

But let me now quote a few passages in which the committees were able to provide particularly felicitous readings. I mentioned earlier that we had worked through one version concerning the establishment of the cities of refuge. Consider now portions of Joshua 20 to see how well the committee managed:

> Then the LORD spoke to Joshua, saying, "Say to the Israelites, 'Appoint the cities of refuge, of which I spoke to you through Moses, so that anyone who kills a person without intent or by mistake may flee there; they shall be for you a refuge from the avenger of blood. The slayer shall flee to one of these cities and shall stand at the entrance of the gate of the city, and explain the case to the elders of that city; then the fugitive shall be taken into the city, and given a place, and shall remain with them. And if the avenger of blood is in pursuit, they shall not give up the slayer, because the neighbor was killed by mistake, there having been no enmity between them before.

One can see that the parties are very well identified, that the language is inclusive, and that, even if it was the case that women did not use the institution of cities of refuge, the language does not falsify that fact.

The NRSV of the Sermon on the Mount also has excellent instances of inclusivity. See, for example, Matthew 6:24:

> No one can serve two masters; for a slave will either hate the one and love the other, or be devoted to the one and despise the other. You cannot serve God and wealth.

The saying about the rich (Matt 19:23-24) is also handled well:

> Truly I tell you, it will be hard for a rich person to enter the kingdom of heaven. Again I tell you, it is easier for a camel to go through the eye of a needle than for someone who is rich to enter the kingdom of God.

Job 3 is another instance in which the translators produced a smooth reading:

> Why is light given to one in misery,
>   and life to the bitter in soul,
> who long for death, but it does not come,
>   and dig for it more than for hidden treasures;
> who rejoice exceedingly,
>   and are glad when they find the grave?

Isaiah 2:17 may be a bit less satisfactory:

> The haughtiness of people shall be humbled,
> and the pride of everyone shall be brought low.

IV. REMAINING PROBLEMS

But problems clearly remain. Have we adequately
addressed the language that gives trouble and offense to
others who take exception to certain forms of reference?
We have eliminated "dumb" in favor of "speechless" or
the like, and we have rarely used the term "leper" but in
the Old Testament have referred to persons with "a leprous
disease," with a note indicating that several kinds of skin
disease are covered by the biblical term often translated
"leprosy." But we probably are on the threshold of new
forms of reference to persons with handicapping condi-
tions, and it will be wise now to begin to collect references
that can be used in a forthcoming revision.

More critical are such terms for the Deity as "Lord,"
which the NRSV continues to print in small capital letters
when the personal name for the Deity, YHWH, appears in
the text. We did not consider long enough, perhaps, the
question whether there might be a more suitable term than
"LORD" for the Tetragrammaton. We did briefly consider
the term chosen by James Moffatt in his translation of the
Bible, "the Eternal," but there was no real support for its
adoption. We talked of using "the Sovereign," but that
seemed no more suitable than "the LORD." We needed "the
Creator" for those occurrences of just that term in the
Hebrew. Finally, since we found no better alternative for
"the LORD," we let that familiar term stand.

We were in agreement that we should not eliminate
all the personal pronouns for the Deity, though we did find
that often we could reduce the number of such pronouns
by simply eliminating those that seemed unnecessary. I find
that readers are actually in a rather good position with the
NRSV to make such adjustments in public reading as they

think appropriate, now that the unnecessary masculine references to human beings have been so widely removed. It is a genuine pleasure, as I have had occasion to discover, to be able to read the lessons appointed for the day in such a way as to eliminate entirely masculine references to the Deity, and to do so without having had to retranslate or reproduce the biblical lessons in advance. With only a little practice and nothing but the NRSV in hand, we can hear an English rendering of the NRSV lessons from Torah and Psalter, from Epistle and Gospel, that is genuinely inclusive.

The NRSV has its flaws. Numerous readings are not what one or more of the translators would have preferred. No doubt there are mistakes, instances of lack of consistency, infelicities of expression, and perhaps some howlers. But on the basis of my reexamination of considerable portions of the text I would judge that it is by far our most inclusive Bible, the one best suited for public reading among all the newer translations, and our most accurate available English Bible.

— APPENDIX —

Members of the
Standard Bible Committee

A T THE time of the publication of the New Revised Standard Version of the Bible (September 30, 1990), the membership of the Standard Bible Committee was comprised of the following biblical scholars:

WILLIAM A. BEARDSLEE
Emeritus, Emory University

PHYLLIS A. BIRD
Garrett-Evangelical Theological Seminary

GEORGE W. COATS
Lexington Theological Seminary

DEMETRIOS J. CONSTANTELOS
Stockton State College (New Jersey)

ROBERT C. DENTAN
Emeritus, General Theological Seminary

ALEXANDER A. DI LELLA, O.F.M.
Catholic University of America

J. CHERYL EXUM
Boston College

REGINALD H. FULLER
Emeritus, Virginia Theological Seminary

PAUL D. HANSON
Harvard Divinity School

WALTER HARRELSON
Emeritus, Divinity School, Vanderbilt University

WILLIAM L. HOLLADAY
Andover Newton Theological School

SHERMAN E. JOHNSON
*Emeritus, Church Divinity School
of the Pacific*

ROBERT A. KRAFT
University of Pennsylvania

GEORGE M. LANDES
Union Theological Seminary (New York)

CONRAD E. L'HEUREUX
University of Dayton

S. DEAN MCBRIDE, JR.
Union Theological Seminary (Virginia)

BRUCE M. METZGER
Emeritus, Princeton Theological Seminary

PATRICK D. MILLER, JR.
Princeton Theological Seminary

PAUL S. MINEAR
Emeritus, Yale Divinity School

LUCETTA MOWRY
Emerita, Wellesley College

ROLAND MURPHY, O.CARM.
Emeritus, Duke Divinity School

HARRY M. ORLINSKY
*Hebrew Union College /
  Jewish Institute of Religion*

MARVIN H. POPE
Emeritus, Yale University

J. J. M. ROBERTS
Princeton Theological Seminary

ALFRED VON ROHR SAUER
Emeritus, Christ Seminary — Seminex

KATHARINE D. SAKENFELD
Princeton Theological Seminary

JAMES A. SANDERS
School of Theology at Claremont

GENE TUCKER
Candler School of Theology, Emory University

EUGENE C. ULRICH
University of Notre Dame

ALLEN WIKGREN
Emeritus, University of Chicago

*   *   *

During the sixteen years that the work of revision progressed, four of the members of the committee were taken by death. These were Herbert G. May, Frank W. Beare, George MacRae, S.J., and Bruce Vawter, C.M.

For a listing of all members of the Standard Bible Committee from the beginning (1929) to 1980, see the chapter by Metzger in *The Word of God: A Guide to the English Versions of the Bible,* ed. Lloyd R. Bailey (Atlanta: John Knox Press, 1982), pp. 42-44. In addition to the names listed there and in the list above, the name of Delbert Hillers, Johns Hopkins University, should be mentioned. Hillers served on the committee from 1981 to 1986, when he resigned owing to the press of other work.

Index of Scripture References

90   *Index of Scripture References*